Disclosing Secrets

An Addict's Guide For When, To Whom, and How Much To Reveal

by

**M. Deborah Corley, Ph.D. and
Jennifer P. Schneider, M.D., Ph.D.**

THIS BOOK IS A COMPANION TO *SURVIVING DISCLOSURE: A PARTNER'S GUIDE FOR HEALING THE BETRAYAL OF INTIMATE TRUST*

FOR INFORMATION CONTACT:

M. Deborah Corley, Ph.D.
Sante Center for Healing
914 Country Club Road
Argyle, TX 76226
(800) 258-4250

Jennifer P. Schneider M.D., Ph.D.
3052 N Palomino Park Loop
Tucson, AZ 85712
(520) 990-7886

Please visit our websites at:
www.jenniferschneider.com
www.santecenter.com

Authors' note:
The quotations in this book come from real people but have been edited for clarity and changed to protect the individuals' confidentiality. Some stories and circumstances portrayed in these pages are composite in nature, combined to form illustrative viewpoints, characters and stories. Any resemblance of such composites to any actual persons is entirely coincidental.

ISBN: 1477608281 ISBN 13: 9781477608289

Library of Congress Control Number: 2012910398

CreateSpace, North Charleston, SC

Advance Acclaim for *Disclosing Secrets: An Addict's Guide for What, to Whom, and How Much to Reveal.*

"Clinicians and researchers, Drs. Corley and Schneider in *Disclosing Secrets* offer their wisdom and research findings in a compassionate and insightful way that helps to sort the difficult but critical process of disclosing secrets so necessary in the healing from addiction. Filled with case examples and a well-organized set of steps to disclose secrets, this book is an important ally to recovering addicts as well as the clinicians who treat them."

> **Kenneth M. Adams,** Ph.D., CSAT, Author of *Silently Seduced: When Parents Make Their Children Partners* and *When He's Married to Mom: How to Help Mother-Enmeshed Men Open Their Hearts to True Love and Commitment* and Clinical Director of Kenneth M. Adams and Associates

"Clear, detailed, with many helpful examples. . . *Disclosing Secrets* is an excellent book on the complex subject of revealing sexual secrets—affairs, cybersex, and other compulsive behaviors— to one's partner. Schneider and Corley guide the reader through the inevitable fears, emotions, and uproar that accompany the process of unburdening oneself to one's partner. While truth is inevitably the path to freedom and potential healing, the reader learns to reveal secrets in a conscious, thoughtful way. Read this book and set yourself free."

> **Charlotte Sophia Kasl,** Ph.D. *Women, Sex and Addiction: A Search for Love and Power; If the Buddha Married– Creating Enduring Relationships on a Spiritual Path.*

"Drs. Corley and Schneider have produced, through a lifetime of research and clinical observation, some of the most important insights about the effect secret keeping has on relationships. This book outlines the reasons being honest is the only way to deepen trust, heal betrayal, and, no matter the consequences, a full disclosure makes the true path to healing possible. There is much to learn from this comprehensive study of one of the least understood topics in our field."

Linda Hudson, MS, LPC, Hudson Consulting Associates
Co-author, *Making Advances: A Comprehensive Guide to Treatment of Female Sex and Love Addicts*

"Disclosing secrets is one of the most difficult challenges an addict faces in recovery. Corley and Schneider provide an excellent resource to guide addicts through a stressful, but necessary process. This is an essential guide for any addict considering disclosure."

Stefanie Carnes, PhD, LMFT Author of
Mending a Shattered Heart a Guide for Partners of Sex Addicts and *Facing Heartbreak: Steps to Recovery for Partners of Sex Addicts.*

Disclosing Secrets and *Surviving Disclosure* are comprehensive guides for addicts and their families to do what is most frightening - become honest and transparent to the ones they love. For therapists, these books are invaluable tools to help recovering addicts and their families heal from the destruction of addiction. At Millennium, we use this material not only with clients struggling with sex addiction but with all our clients who are dealing with dishonesty and secrets.

Ann Foster, Founder & President,
Millennium Counseling Center

"*Disclosing Secrets* is by far one of the most important books in the sexual addiction recovery process. Every therapist, sex addict and their partner should read this. Knowing what to say, when to say, and how to say it can help heal the wounded trust that accompanies sexual addiction. I am impressed with the depth of coverage that Schneider and Corley present in this new edition."

Brenda Schaeffer, author
Is It Love or Is It Addiction?

"Filled with practical and varied examples, *Disclosing Secrets* offers wisdom about navigating the frightening and painful path of disclosure. This book is an invaluable aid for both addicts and those who help them. Fantastic!"

Marnie C. Ferree, MA, LMFT, author of
No Stones – Women Redeemed From Sexual Shame

"Those working to heal the wounds brought about through past betrayals, lies and addictive behaviors are well served by the publication of this meaningful guide. The book offers clear direction regarding the oft confusing amends-making part of the recovery process. Kudos to Drs. Corley and Schneider for this important contribution."

Robert Weiss LCSW, CSAT-S
Author, Educator, Sex & Intimacy Disorders Expert,
Elements Behavioral Health

"Jennifer Schneider and Deborah Corley have pioneered in the roller-coaster world of disclosure and brought real help to both addicts and partners. This new version of *Disclosing Secrets* will be appreciated by all involved. A must read for recovering people and their therapists."

Patrick Carnes, Ph.D. Leading author and
researcher in the field of sex addiction

"Revealing the truth about lying, keeping secrets and betraying a partner through addiction can be just as vulnerable as being the one receiving the news. From many years of clinical experience, Corley and Schneider provide tools for the addict to reveal the right information to their partners in the safest possible way. *Disclosing Secrets* helps all three of you: you, your partner and your relationship."

Joe Kort, Ph.D., Founder of The Center for
Relationship and Sexual Health

"Integrity and vulnerability are the heart of all healthy relationships. Corley and Schneider lead the way, assisting couples in developing the courage to embrace these foundational practices, and providing them with a map for the journey. Their work is timely and essential."

Sonnee D. Weedn, Ph.D, Clinical and Forensic Psychologist
Founder of Sonnee Weedn Institute for Integrative Therapy

"Groundbreaking, extremely important work to those confronting disclosure in their relationship. A thoughtful and thorough guide and by far the best on the market! This invaluable book will help avoid pitfalls in the disclosure process and shape a positive and informed outcome for those impacted by sex addiction."

Cara W. Tripodi, LCSW, CSAT-S, Executive Director, STAR/Sexual Trauma & Recovery, Inc.

"Once again Corley and Schneider have written a comprehensive guide to facilitate the disclosure process. This is a book that no therapist should be without and a book that everyone going through the disclosure process should read. Without guidance the process can be devastating, but with help the process will be healing."

Barbara Levinson Ph.D, RN, LMFT, LSOTP, Certified Sex Therapist Diplomate. The Center for Healthy Sexuality, Houston, TX

"Disclosing Secrets is perhaps *the* "go to" work available to therapists working with couples facing the painful and complex process of disclosing various types of betrayal, and specifically sexual betrayal. This exceptionally comprehensive and detailed guidebook answers myriad questions about how, when and why to disclose, to suggestions for healing and rebuilding after disclosure."

Anna Valenti-Anderson, LCSW, LISAC, CSAT Private practice in Phoenix, AZ, specializing in sex, intimacy and codependency.

"Drs. Corley and Schneider have done it again! They've provided two masterfully written, practical and invaluable manuals for those struggling with disclosure. Their newly released addict's guide and the accompanying guide for partners surviving disclosure, offer essential step-by-step guidance for a variety of disclosure circumstances, current research, and "how-to" resources to move beyond the pain and trauma of discovery. These guides are an invaluable "must read" for individuals who are struggling with the distress of sex addiction, disclosure and for professionals who work with couples and sexual infidelity."

Debra L. Kaplan, MA, LAC, LISAC, CSAT-S Private Practice, Tucson, Arizona

"Corley and Schneider, both towering leaders in the field of sex addiction recovery, have updated and improved their already classic book about disclosing secrets by turning it into two companion texts. Both are exceedingly helpful to couples navigating through the painful process of addiction recovery. The chapter on disclosing to children is especially useful in meeting the needs of this vulnerable population. The inclusion of frequently asked questions is especially useful for those seeking the best way to take one of the hardest and most important steps toward healing damaged relationships. There is no better way to approach the disclosure of secrets than this book and its companion for partners."

Bill Herring, LCSW, CSAT
Private Practice, Atlanta, Georgia

"For more than a decade, *Disclosing Secrets* has been the definitive source for those contemplating a disclosure as well as those facilitating disclosures. In this newly updated version, Drs. Deb Corley and Jennifer Schneider use their broad clinical experience to help sex addicts navigate the stormy waters of disclosure. Reading this book is of paramount importance before starting this important journey."

Milton S. Magness, D Min, MA Psy, CSAT
Author of *Thirty Days to Hope & Freedom From Sexual Addiction, Hope & Freedom for Sexual Addicts and Their Partners*, and *I Can Stop* DVD series.

About the Authors

M. Deborah Corley, PhD received her B.A. from the University of Colorado at Colorado Springs and her M.A. and Ph.D. from Texas Woman's University. She is co-founder and co-owner of Santé Center for Healing, a residential treatment center for addictions near Denton, Texas. She serves as clinical consultant to the Santé treatment team and faculty for the courses Santé co-sponsors for professionals with the UT Southwestern Medical School. She won the 2008 Merit Award from Society of the Advancement for Sexual Health (SASH), the 1999 Carnes Award for outstanding achievement in the field of sex addiction and was the co-recipient with Dr. Schneider of the Clinician's Most Valuable Article Award by the American Foundation for Addiction Research in 2003 for their work on disclosure. She is the past president of the Board for SASH and a clinical member of the American Association of Marriage and Family Therapists. Licensed both as an addiction treatment specialist and marriage and family therapist, Deb has over 25 years of experience working with and conducting research on addictive disorders and high risk families. As an international speaker in the US and Canada, her focus on treatment of addictions, trauma resolution, disclosure, interpersonal neurobiology and meeting attachment needs is well received.

Jennifer P. Schneider, M.D., Ph.D received her B.S. from Cornell University, her M.S. and Ph.D. in Human Genetics from the University of Michigan, and her M.D. from the University of Arizona College of Medicine. She is Board Certified in Internal Medicine, certified by the American Society of Addiction Medicine, and is a Diplomate of the American Academy of Pain Management. After practicing Internal Medicine for many years, she then specialized in treating patients who were living with chronic pain. In addition, for over 25 years she has been a researcher, speaker, and author in the field of compulsive sexual disorders, with a special interest in the effect of sex addiction on the family. Dr. Schneider has been Associate Editor of the journal *Sexual Addiction & Compulsivity* for many years, and has authored many articles, book chapters, and several books in the field. In 1998 she won the

Patrick Carnes Award for lifetime contribution to the sex addiction field and in 2007 the SASH Award for lifetime contributions to research in the sex addiction field.

Other Books by the Authors

By M. Deborah Corley:

Making Advances: A Comprehensive Guide to Treatment of Female Sex and Love Addicts, edited by Marnie Ferree, 2012.

Embracing Recovery from Chemical Dependence, with Jennifer P. Schneider and Richard Irons, 2003.

Disclosing Secrets: When, to Whom, and How Much to Reveal, with Jennifer P. Schneider, 2002

By Jennifer P Schneider:

The Myth of the Jewish Race, with Raphael Patai, 1976.

Back From Betrayal: Recovering from his Affairs, Third Edition, 2005.

Sex, Lies, and Forgiveness: Couples Speak on Healing From Sex Addiction, with Burt Schneider, Third Edition, 2004.

The Wounded Healer: Addiction-sensitive Approach to the Sexually Exploitative Professional, with Richard Irons, 1999

Embracing Recovery from Chemical Dependence, with M. Deborah Corley and Richard Irons, 2003.

Disclosing Secrets: When, to Whom, and How Much to Reveal, with M. Deborah Corley, 2002

Untangling the Web: Breaking Free from Sex, Porn, and Fantasy Addiction in the Internet Age, with Robert Weiss, 2006

Living with Chronic Pain, Second Edition, 2009.

Acknowledgments

We would like to thank all the addicts and partners who have participated in our research over the years, as well as those clients who have given permission to use their original work. We too would like to thank Bill Herring for his input on our surveys for the Disclosure of Relapse research, Joshua Hook, PhD from University of North Texas for help with data analysis, David Delmonico, Ph.D. from Duquesne University for help securing the IRB approval for human subject research, Charlotte Kasl, Ph.D. for help with editing the manuscript, and Robert Kafes and Debra Kaplan for their review of the FAQs. Special thanks go to Marni Dittmar, librarian at Tucson Medical Center Medical Library, for facilitating library research in the field.

To our daughters

Contents

Preface

It is our honor to write a preface to *Disclosing Secrets: An Addict's Guide for When, To Whom, and How Much to Reveal* and *Surviving Disclosure: A Partner's Guide for Healing the Betrayal of Intimate Trust*. No two people are better suited to write these tandem books than Dr. M. Deborah Corley and Dr. Jennifer Schneider. In 2002 they wrote *Disclosing Secrets,* a book which is still actively used by professionals working with those who have crossed inappropriate sexual boundaries.

In the book focused on disclosing, Drs. Corley and Schneider provide very specific and helpful step-by-step suggestions about if, when, and how to disclose. The book entitled, *Surviving Disclosure: A Partner's Guide for Healing the Betrayal of Intimate Trust* is a groundbreaking tool. It provides comprehensive and yet detailed information for partners facing the very difficult process of receiving a disclosure. Each book does a wonderful job of identifying the challenges facing each individual as well as the process of healing.

Those needing to disclose and their partners will appreciate Dr. Schneider and Dr. Corley creating two books with similar information. In a typically emotional process, knowing your partner is receiving similar information that is catered to their specific needs can be comforting and avert adding to the difficulty of the process. Readers will find the authors do not simply provide answers. Instead, those considering disclosing and whether to receive a disclosure are given multiple perspectives and case examples to aid them in deciding whether to proceed with the process of disclosure. Particularly helpful is the special emphasis throughout the books placed upon spouses or significant others, and children. The chapter entitled, "Reveal Now or Save the Worst for Later: The Pain of Staggered Disclosure" hits the nail on the head regarding very important information for the addict to address. They have done a wonderful job of integrating relevant research, clinical knowledge and case studies throughout these two books.

The authors go beyond simply addressing disclosure between two individuals and review other types of disclosures (e.g., a friend's spouse is having an affair) and special issues (e.g., sex offender registry) as well. The books culminate with a chapter offering practical and direct information on what to do following disclosure, a piece often overlooked by those facing this process. The final chapter is for helping professionals. In addition to being a helpful tool for professionals, this particular chapter can be useful for those entering the process in finding a professional knowledgeable about disclosure or increasing the awareness of a trusted therapist. Each book has an appendix addressing frequently asked questions, providing a tremendous resource for both therapists and clients. Dr. Corley and Dr. Schneider have left no stone unturned in their effort to create a safe and humane process for disclosing very difficult and painful information.

At Psychological Counseling Services, we shall provide these books as a tool for clients. One provides a road map for those needing to disclose and supports them in having the courage to do so through a detailed and caring process. The other provides partners who are understandably hurt, angry, and confused, the information and support they desperately need to negotiate the process of disclosure. Dr. Schneider and Dr. Corley provide much needed information to limit the trauma associated with the disclosure process. We want to thank Deborah Corley and Jennifer Schneider for providing a carefully thought through and sensitive resource for the general public as well as professionals.

Marcus R. Earle, Ph.D., LMFT, CSAT
Ralph H. Earle, M.Div., Ph.D., LMFT, A.B.P.P., CSAT

Introduction

Over a decade ago, we wrote a workbook on disclosure for addicts and their partners. After feedback from therapists, addicted persons and partners, we decided that we wanted to have a book for addicts and a separate one for partners because the experience of disclosure is so different for each.

This book is written for addicts who've been keeping secrets that they are now ready or are being encouraged to reveal. It is also a guide-book for healing. It contains information about how to hold onto, repair, and grow a relationship after disclosure. The companion book for partners – *Surviving Disclosure: A Partner's Guide for Healing the Betrayal of Intimate Trust* is available at www.amazon.com.

Revealing his or her behaviors is one of the most difficult steps an addict takes on the road to recovery. Much thought, care, and planning should go into any disclosure. The meaning of a disclosure is differ-ent for the addict who is new to recovery than it is for one who has relapsed. The meaning is different for the partner or other recipients of the revelations than it is for an addict. Behaviors that are illegal or put at risk the health or the finances of a household or company make the timeliness of telling even more important. Matters are complicated further by the number and ages of children, the state of finances and health, years invested in a marriage and in some cases for sex addicts, if other children are the result of sexual behavior outside the marriage. However, a disclosure indefinitely postponed or thoughtlessly carried out can be as destructive as the addictive behavior itself.

Of the many people who donated their time and energy to complete surveys and interviews in our earlier research and to those in our most recent study we are grateful. The participants were recovering from substance use disorders, food addiction, out-of-control spending, Internet and cybersex addiction and other psychiatric disorders. All identified themselves as having difficulty with sexual addiction. We believe that you, our readers, will find the book useful no matter what your addiction history. In fact, people who are not addicted but want to disclose in a healthy way a secret such as a child out of wedlock or childhood abuse, will also find this book helpful.

Both men and women can become addicted. Most of the time, we use the words addict and partner to denote two people in a coupled relationship. If a pronoun is used to identify the addict, we may use either he or she. We mean for this book to help people in all types of relationships, not just those in a heterosexual marriage. We use the term relationship, coupleship, and marital relationship to reflect a committed relationship that exists or is being formulated between two people. We try to make a distinction if we are talking about a parent-child relationship, patient-physician, supervisor-employee, or some other type of specific relationship.

If you have been in recovery for a while, you have undoubtedly had to reveal secrets. As a result of the reaction by the person you told, you may have a great deal of fear and be ambivalent about what to say if you are facing disclosure again. This book will provide you with a blueprint for further disclosure, and will help you understand what information is advisable to tell and what to keep private. You will be able to negotiate the turbulent waters of disclosure in a more knowledgeable and informed way. You will have a better awareness of the support you and your partner need, have guidelines for how much and when to divulge, and ways for helping stabilize and maintain your relationship after you've opened yourself up.

The book is organized into three sections. The first section, Chapters One through Four, looks at the power of disclosure – the shame and fear you have lived with, the relief of unburdening yourself, and the healing power of the truth. We describe a variety of situations where people have kept secrets and told lies, but are faced with the need to acknowledge their behavior. This section discusses why people decide to reveal secrets, the wide range of reactions and consequences, and how to determine what type of disclosure is right for you.

The middle section, Chapters Five through Eight, tell you how to go about doing a variety of types of disclosures. Chapter Five outlines a step-by-step approach to doing a formal disclosure including what, if anything, to keep private. Most people have questions about what to tell the children – even adult children – and that information is in Chapter

Six. It is common for addicted people to relapse, and acknowledging a slip or relapse is a serious issue. Chapter Seven provides tips for what to do when there is a relapse, how to handle other disclosures when the addict remembers something else, setting and maintaining boundaries, testing for sexually transmitted diseases, atonement, and coping. Finally, Chapter Eight speaks to special issues that sometimes exist and decisions that need to be made about what to say at work, what to do if the media gets involved, or what to tell people in your faith community or others outside your immediate family.

The final section, Chapters Nine and Ten, tell you how to proceed after disclosure as well as how a therapist can best help you with divulging your compulsive behaviors. Chapter Nine addresses what to do next after disclosure. You will also learn what do to if your partner wants a period of separation, is very angry, and threatens you. This chapter also provides suggestions for healing and forgiveness. Every situation provides an opportunity to be one's best self and learn from the experience. Ways to learn the lessons are located in this chapter.

The final chapter, Chapter Ten, is really for professionals who are helping addicts and partners work through the process of disclosure. Although we believe this book will help any addicted person with this process, disclosure often generates strong emotions that not everyone is able to manage. We strongly encourage you to seek the help of a trained professional to help you. If you are already working with someone, this chapter may be of help to them.

Although this book is for all people in recovery, we offer material specific to sexual addiction in each chapter and in the two appendices in the back. Appendix A contains Frequently Asked Questions about Disclosing Sexual Secrets while Appendix B lists Recovery Resources. Excruciating as disclosure is, it's a process that can strengthen and even improve a relationship. Disclosing secrets is always difficult. With this book, the process can become an opportunity for healing. We hope you will take that opportunity now.

MDC and JPS

Chapter One

The Power of Disclosure: Why People Tell

Jay, a previously married 40-year-old salesman, had had a string of affairs along with cocaine use; his first wife eventually left him. He hoped to do better by Monica, but within a year of their wedding he had already racked up two brief affairs. He rationalized that his problem "wasn't all that bad, he could control things" because he had used only alcohol, not cocaine, during the short-term affairs. The crisis came after three years of marriage, when Sue, his latest affair partner, threatened to tell Monica about the relationship. Jay decided to tell Monica before she would hear the bad news from Sue. Monica was devastated. Knowing about Jay's history of cheating in his first marriage, she asked him about any other affairs during their three years together, and was distraught to learn that there had been two others.

Monica and Jay's marriage survived his affairs and excessive drinking with the help of addiction counseling, couples' therapy, and Twelve-Step mutual-help meetings for sex and alcohol addiction. Years later, remembering the anger and pain she'd felt at learning of Jay's affairs, Monica recalled that the single most important factor that made her willing to stay in the marriage was Jay's decision to reveal his secret life to her before she heard it from Sue. What this decision meant to Monica was that she and their marriage were important enough to Jay that he would become honest with her. He was willing to risk losing her in order to save the marriage, and this was very powerful to Monica.

This book is about secrets kept by addicts. It is also about the secrets parents, children, friends, and others keep in hopes that if no one talks about the secret, it doesn't exist. This book is also about lies, which protect secrets; about disclosure, which is how people reveal secrets;

and about forgiveness, which is how painful secrets, once revealed, get processed and ultimately lose their ability to wound.

Not all secrets are bad. Secrets can sometimes enhance intimacy. A partner who chooses to share something special and private about herself that no one else knows makes you feel special and can strengthen the bond between you. Intimacy is the willingness to be vulnerable to another person, to open up to him or her knowing that your partner has your best interest at heart. Transparency is the basis of connection. However, sometimes, not telling a secret is the kindest and most appropriate thing to do when someone's physical or emotional health is fragile or if the person lacks the intellectual capacity or maturity to understand the information. It is also wise to keep a secret when revealing it risks violence. But most people keep secrets because they are afraid. They fear that if the truth is known, something bad will happen – such as the partner will leave them or shame them.

Yet people do decide to disclose.

Why Addicts Disclose

Sometimes addicts disclose because they feel so ashamed and guilty that the guilt overwhelms them, so they tell. Others are forced to tell because some authority (such as the law, a boss, a friend, or a therapist) insists on it, and they figure it is better to do damage control than have the partner hear about their addiction from someone else. Sometimes people tell because they think it is the right thing to do—they are trying to be congruent with their values, and deep down, they value honesty over lying even if they haven't always told the truth. This is especially true for people who are in addiction recovery and are trying to rebuild the relationship on a foundation of honesty or when starting new relationships. By opening up in a heartfelt way, the addict honors the partner and knows that the partner is making a choice based on truth and honesty. The partner in turn is likely to feel relieved and more hopeful.

Other addicts break under the intense scrutiny of a partner, therapist, employer, or police and tell because they are tired of keeping the lie or don't see any other way out.

In cases in which a partner's health could be harmed with a sexually transmitted disease, or if a pregnancy is a possibility (especially if the pregnancy is from another relationship outside the marriage), people divulge because they feel they owe it to their partners. Protecting their partner from a health risk is more important than are other consequences of telling.

Like Jay in the example above, some people tell because they got caught or someone else threatened to tell. Sometimes they feel they have no choice, or they open up out of obedience or because they hope this will be the end of the pain they are experiencing as a result of carrying the burden of the secret. Others disclose because they are members of a Twelve-Step program of recovery, a program that recommends rigorous honesty as a cornerstone of sobriety. Yet sometimes the advice from the Twelve- Step program is a bit confusing, leaving the addict wondering whether to acknowledge his compulsive behavior. Often the reactions of the partner are not what they expected. Take John's case:

John, a 33-year-old stockbroker with a three-year history of cocaine addiction, hit bottom after a particularly intense binge and went into treatment. As is true for many cocaine addicts, his sexual appetite had been sent into high gear by the drug, and for several months sexual activities with prostitutes had accompanied his cocaine use. John's wife, Ellen, knew he was going into treatment for cocaine, but she was unaware of the frequent cocaine-sex connection and had no idea he'd been seeing prostitutes. (There is also a methamphetamine-sex connection as with many other stimulants, making sobriety a real challenge.)

At the treatment center, John's counselor, Larry, told him that recovery requires rigorous honesty. "We're only as sick as our secrets," he intoned, opening up the Big Book of Alcoholics Anonymous to page 58. There John read "Those who do not recover are people who cannot or will not completely give themselves to this simple program, usually men and women who are constitutionally incapable of being honest with themselves"—and with others, Larry added. Larry encouraged John to divulge that he had had unprotected sex with the prostitutes and had put his wife's health in danger by then having sex with her. "Keeping such a big secret will poison your recovery," he cautioned

John as he left him alone with the Big Book. "Plus your wife has the right to know so she can protect her own health."

John remembered the time he'd come home late smelling of perfume. He had thought to cover the alcohol smell with a breath mint, but did not think about the perfume. Ellen had immediately noticed the unusual scent and confronted John. "Have you been with another woman?" she demanded.

John had learned that the best defense was a good offense: "No, of course not! You're supposed to be my best friend, not my interrogator! No wonder I don't like to come home! When you start acting nicer, I'll be more interested in spending time with you!"

Ellen immediately backed down: "I'm sorry, John, I don't know what got into me. I go crazy when I even think of you with another woman. I just couldn't stand it. If you ever had sex with someone else, I'd have no choice but to leave you. I couldn't bear it. It would be the end of our marriage."

Later, John thought about Larry's words, and then Ellen's threat to leave if he ever had sex with someone else, so he felt he couldn't possibly tell Ellen about the prostitutes. He idly turned the pages of the Big Book, until suddenly the words on page 81 jumped out at him: "After a few years with an alcoholic, a wife gets worn out, resentful and uncommunicative. . . . The husband begins to feel lonely, sorry for himself. He commences to look around in the nightclubs, or their equivalent, for something besides liquor. Perhaps he is having a secret and exciting affair with 'the girl who understands.'" Boy that fit his story—there was no pressure with a prostitute. "The guy who wrote this knew what he was talking about!" John thought. He read on, "Whatever the situation, we usually have to do something about it. If we are sure our wife does not know, should we tell her? Not always, we think. If she knows in a general way that we have been wild, should we tell her in detail? Undoubtedly we should admit our fault. She may insist on knowing all the particulars. She will want to know who the woman is and where she is. We feel we ought to say to her that we have no right to involve another person. We are sorry for what we have done and, God willing, it shall not be repeated. More than that, we cannot do."

John thought, "This was more like it! The founders of AA were recommending against telling her anything more than she already knew!" John began seriously reading the Big Book, looking for more support. He found it on page 124: "We know of situations in which the alcoholic or his wife has had love affairs. In the first flush of spiritual experience they forgave each other and drew closer together. . . Then, under one provocation or another, the aggrieved one would unearth the old affair and angrily cast its ashes about … and they hurt a great deal … In most cases the alcoholic survived this ordeal without relapse, but not always. So we think that unless some good and useful purpose is to be served, past occurrences should not be discussed."

Though a bit confused by the Big Book's words, especially when he thought about what his counselor said, John chose to say nothing to his wife to be on the safe side. After discharge from the treatment center, he joined Cocaine Anonymous (CA) and began working a Twelve-step program. For two months he did well, until one night an old using buddy offered him some cocaine, just for "old time's sake." Suddenly he felt an urge to visit a prostitute, and justified it by telling himself that it was the lesser of two evils, not as risky as using cocaine. However, sitting in the hotel room with her, he felt an irresistible desire to snort cocaine, and suddenly recovery seemed very distant and unimportant. Three days and a lot of cocaine later, John realized he had a second problem. John couldn't stay clean unless he also stayed away from prostitutes, and it was hard for him to give them up. A friend at the CA meeting suggested he check out a Twelve-step program for compulsive sexual behavior, so John began attending Sex Addicts Anonymous (SAA) meetings.

Once again faced with the problem of what to tell his wife, John appealed this time to the book *Hope and Recovery*, a Twelve-step guide for sex addicts considered by many to be analogous to the Big Book of AA for alcoholics. The recovering addicts who authored *Hope and Recovery*, like the authors of the Big Book, advise waiting to tell the partner until one has first discussed it with the group, prayed about it, and felt it was the right time to do so. "Some of us found that it was helpful to have our sponsors with us when we told our partners about our addiction. And if our partners also happened to be in recovery, it was helpful to have their sponsors present too. . . . We wrote down exactly what we wanted to say to our partners and shared it with other addicts first." (p. 97).

Armed with this advice, John chose to wait to tell Ellen, telling himself he needed to find a good sponsor and wanted to find out what others did in SAA as well as CA. However, he did not have a chance to tell her on his own schedule, because two months later Ellen found his copy of *Hope and Recovery*, as well as an SAA meeting schedule, in his car and insisted on a full explanation. By now, four months had elapsed since John had initially gone to the treatment center, and Ellen was extremely angry about having been kept in the dark for so long about his sexual acting out. During those four months, Ellen had continued being sexual with John, and her fear and anger about the possibility of exposure to HIV or other sexually transmitted disease added fuel to the flame. She felt she could not forgive John for continuing to risk her life by having unprotected sex with her after being sexual with prostitutes. Overwhelmed by anger, despair, fear, and distrust, Ellen asked John to leave.

John could have greatly benefited by going to see a knowledgeable therapist after his discharge from the addiction treatment center, a therapist who could have addressed with John his shame and fears and helped him sort out the confusion he felt from the mixed messages he was receiving about disclosure. The therapist could have helped him plan a formal disclosure early on. Had he seen a counselor, this story might have had a happier ending.

Addicts Often Cannot Tolerate Emotional Distress

Daniel Goleman, in his book *Emotional Intelligence* (2006), points out that people who are emotionally intelligent are able to identify their feelings and tolerate how they and the people around them feel. A person who is emotionally competent can identify not only how he or she is feeling, but can identify the feeling states of those around them and respond appropriately.

We learn how to handle strong feelings of anger, sadness, hurt, and sadness, as well as how to attach to others in relationships from our primary caregivers, according to Daniel Siegel (1999). Unfortunately, many addicts did not learn these important lessons because in childhood they experienced trauma and neglect. Addicted people have difficulty managing their feelings, as John demonstrates in the above example. Addicts' strategy for controlling their impulses and altering uncomfortable emotional states involves numbing out, going to extremes, using some substance or engaging in a harmful behavior or both in order to change how they feel. John demonstrates this unhealthy strategy. However, unlike many people whose revelations are precipitated by discovery of the affair or other secret, John had the opportunity to choose the timing and method of disclosure. Sadly, confused by the mixed input he got from his counselor at the treatment center and the recovery books he read, and guided by his motivation to reduce his anxiety and shame rather than to do the responsible thing regarding the risk to his wife's health, he found reasons to repeatedly postpone telling her, until eventually the delay itself became the major problem. He was motivated by fear and rationalized that an early disclosure would result in something bad happening.

Addiction and Honesty: The Impact of the Twelve-Step Philosophy of Disclosure

Alcoholics Anonymous (AA) and its many offshoots are the best-known approach to addiction recovery in the U.S. and many other countries. AA provides group support, new friends to replace former "using" buddies, and a program to not only keep members sober, but also to improve their emotional and spiritual health. Its primary tenets are summarized in a program of twelve steps that group members study and follow. Addicts attend meetings with other addicts, read recovery literature, and "work the Steps," with the help of a Sponsor, who is someone with longer time in recovery and greater experience in living a sober life. Working the Steps is a lengthy process, which can take many months.

Addicts are told that honesty and accountability are important for recovery. The eighth of the Twelve Steps of AA states, "We made a list of all persons we have harmed, and became willing to make amends to them all." The purpose of the Eighth Step is to identify individuals who have been harmed by the addict's behavior as well as assigning ownership of responsibility for the addict's behavior. By preparing to make amends, the addict begins the process of releasing guilt in order to make a fresh start. Actually making the amends constitutes Step Nine. Making a formal amends as part of an addict's step work, though related, is not the same thing as disclosing secrets that are contaminating relationships and/or putting someone's health at risk. This is especially important to recognize because it may be many weeks or months before a recovering addict is ready to carry out Step Nine.

Step Nine cautions the addict who is about to reveal "all": "We made amends to such people wherever possible, except when doing so would injure them or others." We have already mentioned that in a few situations it is indeed better not to tell, but not often. For the addict, fear of hurting the partner and fear of the partner's response is a common reason to minimize the disclosure or simply not tell the truth. Sometimes it is difficult to sort out whether you are holding on to the secret because you believe your partner truly can't handle it, or because you are afraid of being left or other consequences.

We think it is also important to look at the facts behind the life of the author of the Big Book, Bill Wilson—or as most people refer to him, Bill W. In a biography of Bill Wilson, author Francis Hartigan (2000) reports that Bill may have been sober from alcohol, but seems to have struggled with other addictive and compulsive behaviors all his life. He writes, "Bill was compulsive, given to emotional extremes. Even after he stopped drinking, he was still a heavy consumer of cigarettes and coffee. He had a sweet tooth, a large appetite for sex, a major enthusiasm for LSD." Hartigan goes on to say, "Judging from the guilt and remorse he suffered over his inability to control his sexual impulses, even his infidelities seem to be evidence not of a lack of standards but of a failure to live up to them." In addition to his many sexual conquests, Bill also had a long-term affair with a woman named Helen Wynn, to whom he left part of the Big Book royalties. He felt both guilty about the affair and obligated to Helen as well as his wife Lois.

Bill Wilson had a huge impact on alcohol recovery by founding Alcoholics Anonymous, yet one has to wonder what influence his "womanizing" had on his advice in the Big Book not to divulge to one's partner about sexual infidelities. Perhaps Bill was afraid to tell Lois for fear that she would leave after having been put through so much already. Like many addicts, Bill W. often underestimated his wife and her ability to cope.

Thinking your partner can't handle it is a cop-out; it is really slighting your partner. Taking the approach that your partner can't handle it only further hurts your partner. The results of our research overwhelmingly indicate that **partners want to know.** Addicts often lie in such a way as to make their partners feel crazy. By revealing the secrets through disclosure, the addict allows the partner to regain her or his sanity. If you are worried for your partner, then make sure you have thought through how you are going to tell and have a therapist available to help.

Different addicts have dealt with this dilemma in different ways: Bill Wilson chose to say virtually nothing to Lois, and continued having affairs for the rest of his life. Reportedly he never could hold onto good feelings about himself. Like Bill, some addicts never reveal affairs or sexual acting out. Others tell everything, or all the information that their partner asks for. Still others reveal the basic behaviors but not the details. Each of these choices has different consequences for the addict and the partner. (In Chapter 5, we will provide specific information on how to disclose as well as samples of disclosures.)

Will the Truth Help?

The Bible says that the truth will set you free (John 8:32). All religions value honesty as a character trait and expect honesty as a sign of a covenant (a biding or solemn agreement). Honesty is part of being trustworthy and trustworthiness is one of the most widely desired characteristics of a potential partner in a relationship (Gottman, 2011). In most marriages the covenant of honesty is usually an expectation, even if not voiced.

Our research has supported this speculation. We found that the betrayal felt by partners is as much about the lying and secret keeping as about the actual behavior. We also learned that the best chance that a relationship will survive compulsive sexual behavior is if the addict becomes honest and transparent. This is especially true when the behavior disclosed constitutes a relapse.

The whole truth for the first time, although extremely difficult, feels like a kind of freedom. For the first time, you no longer have to hide, hold your breath, wait for the next shoe to drop. You no longer have to live a double life. You can begin to breathe again. You no longer have to feel guilty. This freedom is the power of disclosure. Of course, how you feel depends also on the consequences of telling, but over time most addicts report that, despite the consequences, they are glad they told.

All addicts who are holding onto a major secret face a dilemma of when and how much to tell. When the secret is sexual, keeping it within can be very destructive. Frank Pittman (1989) defines infidelity as "a breach of the trust, a betrayal of a relationship, a breaking of an agreement." In other words, infidelity isn't only about the sexual behavior itself: The dishonesty about the infidelity involves loss of self-esteem, breaking an important commitment to your partner and your relationship, and the energy of keeping the secret that is taken from the relationship. Pittman states that dishonesty may be a greater violation of the rules than the affair or misconduct, and acknowledges that more marriages end as a result of maintaining the secret than do in the wake of telling. He speculates that the partner may be angry, but will be angrier if the affair continues and the partner finds out later. Our research has supported this speculation. We found that the betrayal felt by partners is as much about the lying and secret keeping as about the actual behavior. We also learned that the best chance that a relationship will survive compulsive sexual behavior is if the addict becomes honest and transparent. This is especially true when the behavior disclosed constitutes a relapse.

Although not all addicts are sex addicts or have been sexually unfaithful, they have been unfaithful in that the drug or addictive behavior becomes the primary relationship in their lives. It is as if the person has an affair with the drug. It becomes the most important thing in his or her life and the addict will put the drug or behavior before family, job, community, and all other meaningful relationships.

Emily Brown (1991) concurs that, in most circumstances, the unfaithful person must tell the partner if healing is to occur. When an affair remains secret, all communication between the partners is gradually impaired. The same is true when the affair is with a drug. Ms. Brown advises that behaviors from previous relationships or from long ago do not always have to be revealed. She agrees with our assessment that before actual rebuilding of the relationship can occur, time and support for the partner are necessary and that therapy sessions often take longer or are more frequent to help the partner express her or his anger and sadness about the infidelity.

Reasons for Telling

Telling Because of Health Risks

When a person is diagnosed with Hepatitis C (transmitted sexually or through dirty needles) or a sexually transmitted disease or infection (STD/STI) that is reportable to the state's Health Department, a representative will notify all parties who have potentially been exposed. Many people disclose because they realize that the partner will be notified or that it is necessary for the partner to get medical care.

This is even more important because of the risk of acquiring HIV, still a serious and potentially fatal disease. Because of this risk, more therapists are now insisting on disclosure to the partner of extramarital sexual behaviors or intravenous (IV) drug use. We have found that one of the actions that are most difficult for the partner to forgive is when the addict practices unsafe sex or uses unclean needles for IV drugs and continues to knowingly expose the partner to the risk of contracting a serious illness. Many partners consider this action to signify such lack of caring that they are never able to overcome it and choose instead to end the marriage.

Also of concern to therapists is when an addict engages in behaviors that put him and his family in danger. Purchasing drugs and sex from armed and potentially violent persons, and/or persons who engage in illegal behaviors (for example, drug dealers and prostitutes) not only brings the risk of Hepatitis C, HIV and other STDs, it also brings the risk of potential violence into a household. Police raids and attacks from revenge-seeking spouses are possibilities when persons with unsavory lifestyles are brought into someone's life. Threats from such persons may precipitate disclosure by the addict in an attempt to forestall the potential violence.

On the other side of the coin, a potential health risk that can be the result of disclosure rather than a reason to disclose is domestic violence. This is especially true when it is the wife whose extramarital sexual activities or high-risk drug use have put her husband in danger rather than the other way around. The response of many men to sexual betrayal is extreme anger, which may be directed at the wife, at the affair partner, or both. In the survey reported in *Sex, Lies, and Forgiveness* (2004), several men reported experiencing a murderous rage in response to learning of their wife's extramarital sexual activities. One man displaced his anger onto some furniture, which he chopped to pieces with an axe; another stalked the affair partner, and reported that it was a good thing he did not encounter him alone, or violence would have resulted.

Interestingly, we have found that partners who are themselves recovering addicts tend to be more tolerant upon receiving a sexual disclosure than do partners who are not addicts. We hypothesize that addicts feel guilty about their past behavior and therefore are more willing to forgive it in their partners.

In couples faced with infidelity, both intense jealousy by the male and more tolerance by the female are reported in David Buss's research on jealousy (2000). Buss and other researchers have found that women are more tolerant of sexual affairs than emotional affairs whereas men are just the opposite. Everyone, especially women who are considering divulging material that is likely to be very upsetting to the partner, needs to assess in advance the risk of sustaining physical violence as a result of the disclosure. If there are any concerns about safety, it is imperative to delay disclosure until it can be done in a safe place in the presence of a professional.

Damage Control Disclosure: I'd Better Tell Before Someone Else Does

Robert, a gifted and creative computer programmer who'd been highly paid and highly valued at his company, had always enjoyed print pornography, but when he discovered the many sexual opportunities on the Internet, he was instantly hooked. Because he had a lot of unsupervised time at work, it was easy for Robert to spend an increasing amount of company time on his office computer (as well as out of the office on his iPhone) engaged in viewing pornography, exchanging sexually focused emails and texting with women, and eventually participating in real-time interactive sexual activities. Because Robert's behavior at home did not change, his wife, Laurie, was completely unaware of these activities. Laurie did notice that Robert's interest in sex with her had diminished, but he explained this on the basis that he was working long hours on a complex project at work, and was exhausted by the time he got home.

Unfortunately for Robert, his supervisor walked in on him one day while Robert was involved in online sex. Analysis of Robert's computer and cell phone revealed thousands of stored pornographic images, hundreds of saved personal emails and texts, and evidence of dozens of hours of company time spent in personal sexual activities. Robert's supervisor was already dissatisfied with Robert's diminishing productivity at work, and the incontrovertible evidence he now had of Robert's unauthorized activities gave him the excuse he needed to immediately fire Robert.

Robert was given two hours to pack his belongings. Before the first day was out, a dozen other programmers, including two who were good friends of Robert and Laurie, knew what had happened. Robert went home and told Laurie he'd been fired. "Why?" she asked, incredulous. Robert had to instantly decide how much to tell her. Realizing she was likely to hear it from others the next day, he chose to explain it to her himself first.

A Warning about Cybersex

Some addicts never venture onto the Internet for online sexual activities, but let this be a warning. The Internet has addictive qualities that researchers do not yet fully understand. It is the rare addict that does not get hooked by something on the Net, whether it is gambling, spending out of control, video gaming, chatting, or sharing non-stop emails. In fact, in our most recent study on relapse, 73.5% of respondents stated their relapse involved the Internet. Addicts just have to be careful. Clearly, all online sexual activities (including texting), whether it is playing sexual games, chatting about sexual topics, sending nude or nearly nude pictures of yourself or others, viewing and/or downloading pornography, or viewing another via video streaming, is very addictive for a brain already "wired" for addiction.

It has been estimated that 70 percent of online sexual activities take place between 9 A.M. and 5 P.M., meaning they involve work hours and work computers. The number of addicts who download pornography at work or misuse the Internet has made many employers establish policies of intolerance for such behaviors. When you have just been fired for spending work time doing online sex, it is difficult to keep this from your spouse! It's especially difficult if you know that others in the company know the reason and are likely sooner or later to reveal it to her. You realize all too clearly that it's not a question of whether your mate will find out, but when. In such a setting, it is wiser to tell your mate yourself than to wait until she hears it from someone else; in this way, you have some possibility of presenting the information in the best possible light. Unfortunately, in the interest of "damage control," too many people omit the most hurtful or egregious details. Although such a choice may seem like the most comfortable one initially, our research has shown that it can cause great difficulty later on.

The strategy of "telling it first" is most likely to be used when public disclosure is imminent or legal action is involved, such as being arrested for illegal drug use or possession of a controlled substance; driving while under the influence or while intoxicated; sexual behavior such as soliciting a prostitute, exposing oneself, sex with a minor, or voyeurism; or having a patient lodge a complaint against a physician, dentist, or therapist for engaging in a sexual encounter. The arrest report becomes public record, and the news media frequently look at these records seeking sensational stories. Clearly the spouse will find out about the conduct. Nothing is to be gained by the addict's withholding the information from the partner. Indeed, therapists frequently tell addicts and others that it will be better for them if this information comes directly from them rather than from some other source. Nonetheless, it is common for addicts to minimize and excuse their conduct, and to omit acts of very significant misconduct, about which the spouse learns only later.

I'll Do Anything to Save This Relationship – Including Disclosure

Yet another motivation for revealing sexual behaviors to the partner is a desire to salvage the relationship. When the partner recognizes that this is the motivation of the disclosure, opening up can be the first step to rebuilding trust for the couple. Research has shown that this intent to try to save the marriage is directly related to eventual forgiveness by the betrayed partner (Finket & Rusbult, 2002).

If you recall Jay and Monica, whose story began this chapter, Jay decided to come clean with Monica about his affair with Sue after Sue threatened to tell Monica herself. Jay weighed the risks and benefits of disclosure and decided he had a better chance to save the marriage if Monica heard the bad news directly from him rather than from his affair partner. Upon learning of the affair, Monica had a mixture of reactions, among them anger, hurt, and the painful realization that she would have to construct a new picture in her head of the reality of her recent relationship with Jay. A series of confusing events came to her mind, and she recognized that Jay's ongoing affair might have contributed to her confusion.

For example, Monica remembered a recent excursion with Jay to the Great Smoky Mountains, a vacation she'd really looked forward to but which turned into an emotional disaster. Monica loved hiking and camping, and Jay, who was a city guy at heart, had agreed to spend a long weekend with Monica in the mountains. She felt particularly warm and loving to him at the start of that weekend, and kept telling him how much she loved him—but every attempt to get close to him physically or emotionally was rebuffed by Jay. In fact, he seemed to be going out of his way to be particularly cruel and unpleasant to her. Monica kept wondering all weekend what she had done wrong.

Now, having learned about the affair, Monica asked Jay about what had been going on for him at the time of the camping trip. Reluctantly, he told her he'd been at the height of his affair with Sue, wishing every second that he was with his lover rather than her. Every loving word or gesture by Monica increased Jay's guilt. He kept thinking, "If she only knew how I'm really feeling, she wouldn't think I'm such a caring wonderful husband, she'd realize I'm really worthless." By his uncaring behaviors all weekend, Jay was subconsciously trying to prove to Monica that he didn't deserve her love and positive regard.

Hearing the truth from Jay, painful though it was for her, helped Monica make sense of the recent events in their marriage and validated for her that she wasn't crazy and that her reactions to Jay had been normal. Jay was clearly unhappy to be grilled about these events, but his willingness to answer all her questions suggested to Monica, even in the midst of her anger and pain, that he was committed to their relationship and willing to experience great discomfort in order to try to save the marriage. The power of disclosure is that it gave Monica hope that they might somehow rebuild trust and restore their relationship.

In a group discussion of difficult disclosures, Megan, a 50-year-old artist with three years of recovery from sex addiction, recalled the hardest secret she had to reveal to her husband:

When my daughter Stephanie was conceived, I was in the midst of one of my many affairs. I wasn't sure who was her father—my husband Milt or my affair partner, and I kept my doubts to myself. When Stephanie was seventeen, her high school biology class had a project in which they obtained the blood types of all the kids in the class. I already knew my own blood type and that of my husband, and when Stephanie told me her blood type, I knew for sure that Milt was not her father. I was still having affairs at the time, and I managed to put the new information out of my mind and not think too much about it for the next ten years. But when Milt came for Family Week three years ago when I was being treated for my sex addiction, I knew I had to disclose this awful secret to him. Believe me, it was the scariest thing I'd ever done. Even though by then he knew about the many affairs and seemed committed to sticking by me, I was afraid that this would just be too much for him and that he'd leave me. But he said that as far as he was concerned, Stephanie had always been his daughter and still was. He was angry with me, and also got very depressed, but he worked through it. I also told Stephanie about it at that time. Fortunately, she was 27, an adult with two young children, and she took it pretty well. She already knew about my sex addiction, and she understood that this was part of it. I'm very lucky—I no longer have the burden of this secret, and my husband and daughter have both forgiven me."

References

Alcoholics Anonymous. New York: Alcoholics Anonymous World Services, Inc., 1953

Anonymous. *Hope and Recovery: A Twelve Step Guide for Healing from Compulsive Sexual Behavior*. Center City, MN. 1987.

Brown, Emily. *Patterns of Infidelity*. New York: Brunner Mazel, 1991

Buss, David. *The Dangerous Passion: Why Jealousy Is as Necessary as Love and Sex*. New York: Free Press, 2000.

Finkel, E.J. & Rusbult, C.E. Dealing with betrayal in close relationships: Does commitment promote forgiveness? *Journal of Personal and Social Psychology* 82:956-974, 2002.

Goleman, Daniel. *Emotional Intelligence*. New York: Bantam Books. 2006.

Gottman, John. (2011). *The Science of Trust: Emotional Attunement for Couples*. New York: Norton.

Hartigan, Francis. *Bill W. A Biography of Alcoholics Anonymous Cofounder Bill Wilson.* New York: St. Martin's Press, 2000.

Pittman, Frank. *Private Lies.* New York: WW Norton Co., 1989.

Schneider, Jennifer and Schneider, Burt. *Sex, Lies, and Forgiveness: Couples Speak on Healing from Sex Addiction.* 3rd edition. Tucson, Ariz.: Recovery Resources Press, 2004.

Chapter Two

Secrets and Lies:
Lies Influence Relationships, and Relationships Influence Lies

Why do people lie—that seems pretty obvious doesn't it? They don't want to get in trouble. But it is not that simple for most. Some people speculate that addicts are born liars, but that is not true. We all learn to lie through an important developmental process in which lying serves a specific purpose.

In his book *Lies, Lies, Lies: The Psychology of Deceit* (1996), Charles Ford, MD cites several studies that demonstrate how children use lying. He summarizes:

> *Lying is . . . an essential component in the process of developing autonomy and differentiating oneself from one's parents. The capacity to fool parents demonstrates to children that parents are not omnipotent . . . lying is reinforced (positively or negatively) by the degree to which the child is rewarded or punished for deceitful behavior. (p. 86)*

As children become older, lying provides a way for them to learn that their parents can't totally control them. In this way, the child gains a sense of autonomy. In another example, Ford explains that children use lying to help them in other ways beyond the developmental task of separating self from parents/others. This important distinction relates to an addict's and partner's experiences:

> *If the child experiences repeated trauma (such as sexual abuse, physical abuse, or being raised in a family with an alcoholic parent), lying may become one way to cope with stress. Certainly, putting*

on a false face appears to be one coping mechanism learned when growing up in a family with alcoholism. (p. 86)

Clearly, lying serves an important developmental function as well as a means for coping. Unfortunately, without guidance most addicts fail to learn other ways to gain autonomy and independence in relationships or cope well with adversity or trauma.

Of course, there are other reasons people lie. As we mentioned in Chapter 1, a major reason is to avoid punishment or to punish someone when you are angry. Fooling someone else makes you feel powerful or that you are a part of something. When someone doesn't feel they can ever live up to the expectations of others, that person might lie as a form of self-deception, to maintain their self-esteem, or to accommodate the other person's self-deception. A lie can resolve role conflict or help create a sense of identity. Many times people lie about how they feel to avoid acknowledging the pain they are in.

To keep a secret, you must tell a lie. A lie is a deliberate act in which you either misrepresent or conceal information. There are lies of omission and commission (deliberate lies). There are lies you tell yourself and lies that you tell others. There are lies that are justifiable—for example, to avoid offending someone or to prepare a surprise party for a friend—and there are lies that are toxic. Toxic lies are those addicts use to keep others from learning about their dark side. Toxic lies also violate one's values, ethics, morals, and spiritual beliefs.

As the addict, telling lies helps cover the shame and guilt of knowing that the behavior you have engaged in has harmed you and your partner. Although telling lies is painful, addicts believe that telling the truth will only make things worse. Dishonesty appears to be the lesser of two evils. But the unfortunate result is that lies activate a cognitive process that leads to obsessive thinking about the secret (Wegner& Lane, 1995). Not only do you obsess about your drug or behavior of choice, you now also obsess about how to keep the secrets about your behavior from your partner, family, co-workers, and friends. The obsessing takes up valuable hours each day and night causing loss of productivity by day, insomnia by night. Gradually it builds a wall between you and your partner as it erodes your self-confidence and faith in yourself.

This chapter illustrates several types of secrets guarded by various types of lies and how addicts use and fear the secrets and lies that influence their relationships.

Several Types of Secrets

Secrets that hurt relationships are as common and numerous as are people. Here are a few types of commonly kept secrets that are often triggers for addicts or some partners.

The Emotional Secret

Most addicts were raised in families with emotionally dismissing or disapproving parents. Partners of addicts often find this true for them too. Disapproving parents disregard, ignore, or trivialize a child's painful or negative emotions. At the first sign of emotional distress by their child, a disapproving parent will almost automatically think, "Don't feel—all feelings require something of me that I don't have to give or don't know how to give, so don't feel. If you have a feeling, I will ignore it or tell you it isn't that important." Consequently these children grow up unable to identify the feelings they or others have, or discount their own feeling states.

Dismissing parents reprimand or punish children for emotional expressions. Similar to the disapproving parent, these parents also cannot tolerate the child having an emotional state that they can't control, so the child's response to emotional situations is shut down by threats or punishment. A common response would be, "You better stop that crying before I give you something to cry about!" or "Stop that crying – that cut doesn't hurt!"

Research shows that children raised with these types of parents grow up having a hard time trusting their own judgment. This makes sense. If children are told that their feelings are wrong—that they really don't feel the way they say they feel, then they are likely to grow up believing there is something inherently wrong with them. Unfortunately, the result is someone who can't tolerate emotional distress in himself, herself, or others.

Take Martha who is married to Michael. Martha was raised in an alcoholic family and suffered from low self-esteem. Her father's rages during drinking left her and her siblings afraid to show any emotions. If he was raging, she did everything possible to disappear. She remembered once when her sister started to cry while her father was raging. Her father picked up her sister, slapped her hard across the face, and then shook her for what seemed like forever while yelling for her sister to stop crying. Martha quickly learned it wasn't safe to show any emotions around her father.

When her father wasn't drinking, Martha tried to be the best she could in hopes that she could prevent him from drinking and her mother from getting depressed. Hoping to somehow get her parents to stop their crazy behaviors, she did everything she could to be the "perfect" child. She tried out for school plays and was always given a part, but both parents were too busy to attend. She studied hard in school and was at the top of her class, yet neither of her parents attended her college graduation where she was valedictorian.

Martha felt that no matter what she did, it was not good enough to deserve their love. Working constantly to keep her feelings in check, she behaved kindly to everyone, no matter what they did to her. But before long, she noticed that the people she seemed to attract took advantage of her, asking her to do things that were beyond her capability or her wishes. She continually struggled with her feelings of resentment and frustration that others were taking advantage of her, but feared that if she said anything, they would abandon her. Sometimes, though, when the stress overwhelmed her, she would eat with a vengeance: ice cream, donuts, potato chips—whatever she could get her hands on, bingeing until she thought she'd burst. Then she'd feel so guilty for the feelings and for eating so much that she'd make herself throw up and then run several miles in a day or take laxatives to make sure she did not gain weight. She remembered how when she was a child, her mother complained that she was too fat. Her response was to try even harder to please everyone.

Martha was very surprised when Michael, a medical resident from the hospital where she worked part time, asked her out. She couldn't believe that this good-looking intelligent man would be interested in her.

Michael's background included a prominent Jewish family that looked good on the outside. However, Michael was raised by emotionally dismissing parents. Even though Michael was now over six feet tall and in excellent shape, as a child he was thin and shy. Often last to be chosen on the team, he was frequently taunted and sometimes picked on by the bullies at school. When he would come home crying, he was told to stop acting like a sissy, to stop crying and "be a man." His father was famous for telling him that there was something wrong with him because Michael cried when his dog was hit by a car—that it was just a dog. Michael was then told the story of his father's family's experience during the Holocaust and that Michael was just a spoiled baby trying to use tears to get his way instead of minding his father. Early in his life, Michael vowed never to cry or let himself feel anything again.

Like Martha, Michael set out to make his father proud of him— playing football in the homecoming game despite having a fractured collarbone, working two jobs to save money for college even though his family could easily afford the college tuition, and being in the top quarter of the students in medical school. Yet each time he talked to his father, he was told that he could have done better in some way. Michael felt totally inadequate, but vowed never to show it. Instead he covered it with working harder, being firm with those around him and not giving in to his feelings.

Michael was drawn to Martha like a moth to a flame. People are commonly drawn to mates who they think will provide for them what they missed in childhood. Here was Martha, kind to all the patients, attentive to his stories—laughing and enthusiastic about everything. This clearly was a woman he wanted to marry. She was interested in his work and understanding of his work schedule. She seemed to have no problem rearranging her schedule to fit his so they could be together. She was pretty, smart, and a hard worker herself. She even agreed to raise their children in the Jewish faith. Surely this would please his father.

So Michael and Martha got married. But Michael soon found that his work schedule did not leave much time to be with Martha. After the children were born, she began to focus increasingly on them and complain more and more about why he wasn't home more. He didn't know why she could not see the stress he was under or hear the demands the hospital was making of him. It seemed the harder he worked to bring home a substantial pay check, the more quickly she spent it and the less she was available to him. Over the years she had emotional outbursts during which she would begin to rage, criticizing him for what seemed like everything he did. When he tried to defend himself by saying she was never around when he was at home because she was always out spending the money he made, she would fly off the handle even more or leave in a hysterical fit and refuse to talk to him for days. This scared him so he would just leave the house. It was not long before work was the only place he felt valued. Unable to voice to Martha his fear that he was no longer important to her, he turned to work to make himself feel better. It was at work that a young female intern began to pay attention to him, commenting what a wonderful doctor she thought he was and how grateful she was for all his help. It wasn't long before he was sharing with her his frustrations about the hospital, then about his marriage. This sharing led the intern to believe that there was intimacy between them and she invited him to her apartment for dinner, a nap, and eventually sex.

In the meantime, Martha grew increasingly resentful that she had given up everything of importance to her for him. She saw him working more and more, while being less and less available to her and the children. In the past he at least complained about the demands of work, but he no longer even shared that with her. All he did was demand that the family appear perfect in the community. Unable to talk about her fear that she was no longer important to him, she put all her energy into the children and her volunteer activities. She wanted to punish Michael for his rigidity and isolating behavior, but he would never listen to her unless she was raging. Eventually she would just blow up and shut herself off from him. He would walk out of the house and she would eat to make herself feel better. Then she would put her fingers down her throat, vomiting to keep herself below the petite 95 pounds Michael said he liked.

What a painful existence for both Martha and Michael! Martha's eating disorder was out of control; Michael's work addiction had not been the solution and an affair with an intern was about to make things even worse. As you see, they both feared the same thing—that they were not important to the other person. If each had been able to talk about the pain they were in or hear the other, perhaps they would have been able to create solutions.

Keeping secrets about how they really feel emotionally is a component of all secret-keeping for addicts. This type of secret is usually the one that people are least concerned about, but for most addicts is a catalyst to engage in some behavior that is not good for them or the relationship. Stopping this type of secret keeping is the key to obtaining emotional competence.

The Secret That Isn't a Secret – The Elephant in the Living Room

Sometimes secrets are known, but the unspoken (or sometimes even spoken) rule is to pretend they don't exist. KEEP QUIET, don't rock the boat, don't bring attention to the elephant in the living room. Then you don't have to face the situation. An example is what happens to children in families in which there is ongoing addiction or domestic violence. The children see Mom drunk or simply "not there," perhaps because she is using prescription drugs. Or they see Dad hit the older brother so hard that his nose and mouth bleed and then hear Dad tell him "this is for your own good." These children often pretend that nothing out of the ordinary is happening; they make it their job to do whatever it takes to keep the secret hidden for fear matters will get worse if they tell. They don't invite friends over fearing that the friends will discover the truth about their family. They learn to discount their feelings, and to carry on conversations in which nothing important is ever discussed. They find ways to hide evidence, and frequently take on adult responsibilities far beyond their years. This type of secret-keeping influences both the day-to-day relationships within the family and external relationships.

The normal, healthy development of a child includes opportunities for the child to experience painful and confusing situations. What makes the difference is when a caring adult helps the child identify the feelings he or she is having, validates the feelings, and then helps the child figure out what to do and how to take steps to feel better. But in families where secrets are kept at all costs, children grow up unable to tolerate emotional discomfort. Boundaries are often overly controlling or extremely chaotic, and children have little emotional competence. Later on, such people usually attract someone with a complementary style of relating, so it is no surprise that many addicts choose as a partner an adult child of an addict or victim of some type of abuse or neglect. Such relationships are very likely to quickly include secrets:

Each member of the couple lacks the skills to cope with addiction or traumatic memories, and keeping secrets is already a part of how the couple relates.

The Secret No One Else Knows

Not all secrets exist exclusively between two people. A person can hold onto a secret that no one else knows about. Think about the lesbian teenager who has never told anyone how she feels or thinks about her sexual orientation. The impact on her as an individual intensifies when her parents begin to pressure her during college to get married and give them grandchildren. If this young woman continues to maintain that solitary secret, and fakes attraction to the man she then marries in order to please her parents, not only is her life affected, but so is that of her husband and child.

In a similar situation, John grew up in a strict Catholic family and was expected to marry and have children. Although he regularly dated girls and then women, he knew early in life that he was more attracted to males, but kept this secret. He quickly located other men in his situation on the Internet and soon was meeting other men for anonymous sex. Sometimes he even put himself in danger by having unprotected sex or sex with strangers who seemed so safe on the Internet but who threatened him when they met face to face. On occasion he was beaten and robbed, but told no one and was not able to stop his behavior.

Being what he termed "the favored child," he felt he had to keep quiet about his homosexual behavior. He forced himself to be the best at his job and do what was expected of him not only by his parents but also by the church. He became friends with Jill, a woman who worked in his law firm, and asked her to go out with him. In fact, he felt close to her and soon he asked her to marry him, thinking she would solve the problem of his attraction to men. Of course, he did not tell her his secret. Initially he found sex a novelty and even pleasant with her at first, but later had to fantasize about other men to be able to become aroused enough to be sexual with her.

After the birth of their first son, instead of feeling happy about this event, he was overwhelmed with fear of not living up to the expectations his son might have of him. He sought relief for his anxiety through sex at a rest stop he had heard about online. Unfortunately, this time, the rest stop was a location for a police sting operation. He was arrested the night before his wife was to be released from the hospital. Knowing that she would find out because of the arrest, John felt he had to tell her, but did not know how.

Fear-Based Secrets

At times someone in a family knows the secret but is sworn not to tell for fear that something bad will happen to him or the family. For example, a pre-teen catches his father having sex with someone other than his mother. The father implores the son to keep the secret, for to tell would only hurt his mother. This puts the child in an impossible loyalty conflict, for which there seems to be no way out. If the woman with whom his father is having sex happens to be the wife of a neighbor, this complicates the situation even further for the son.

The Secret Affair

In reality, an affair may be with another person, or a drug, or work, or food, or an image of a person on the Internet. In each example, one person is putting energy into a relationship with someone else or something else and that interferes with the marital relationship. The most painful type of affair is with another person— it represents the betrayal of the spoken or unspoken commitment people make to each other when they agree to be in a relationship. Yes, people can be just as distracted when the "affair" is with food or work—but an affair with another person makes the betrayal feel more personal. It is common for the partner to believe that the reason the addict looked elsewhere was because the partner is somehow not good enough.

Richard was a judge in a mid-sized city. Despite his power in the judicial system, he felt insecure. Over the years he had gained a little weight, really did not like his work, and longed for a more fulfilling career. Richard made a good salary and his wife Rachel liked the money he had and the prestige of being the wife of a judge. Their children were enrolled in the finest private schools, they belonged to the country club, lived in a beautiful home, and drove the best cars, yet he felt he could never please her. He felt stuck. For years, just as he did with his own mother, he felt that no matter what he did, it wasn't enough for his wife. Besides feeling inadequate with Rachel, he also felt she did not understand his need to be creative. For years he had been painting watercolors and at times was convinced he had some talent. But each time he thought of taking a stab at being a professional artist, his wife just laughed and told him to "get real."

For the past few months he had been taking an advanced watercolor course and was really enjoying himself, but had not told Rachel for fear she would disapprove. This was the first time he had been in a class in which he and the other students were encouraged to critique each other's work. To his surprise he had been given very enthusiastic feedback, especially from Tonya, a young woman who shared his love of art. Soon, they began to confide in each other after classes, talking first about their family history, then their disappointment in their respective marriages. Richard began to fantasize about Tonya when he made love to his wife or when he masturbated in the shower. Before long, Richard and Tonya had arranged an out-of-town watercolor workshop together. Richard lied to Rachel about the workshop and told her he would be out of town for business.

While he was on the trip his son broke his leg in a soccer game and Rachel phoned his hotel room to ask him to come home. Tonya answered the phone. They had just ordered dinner in the room after having had sex, so she assumed it was room service. She handed the phone to Richard. Not only was Rachel upset about their son's leg, she was furious about Tonya. He quickly returned home.

After the crisis of the broken leg subsided, Richard realized how much he did love his wife and children, and did not want to lose them. Yet, he thought he also loved Tonya. Rachel confronted him about the "woman's voice" on the phone and demanded to know who she was. Richard minimized his feelings for Tonya but disclosed to Rachel that Tonya was a friend with whom he was only emotionally involved—that his being with her was really nothing and not to take it personally.

Rachel took it personally!

Often other people in the family know or get pulled into the affair. For example, in the movie *Moonstruck*, Cher's character, Loretta, sees her father, Cosmo, out at the opera with a woman with whom he is having an affair. Despite her anger at her father, she enters into the secret with her father rather than risk telling on him because she also has a secret—she is dating and having sex with her fiancé's brother!

As in *Moonstruck*, one lie is used to cover up another. But the guilt and tension are too much for Loretta and Cosmo to tolerate, so over the kitchen table a fight ensues where each tries to minimize their behavior. The emotions that led to the fight are actually generated by the secret.

A person might also use other tactics to reduce the toxic pain of the secret, such as getting sick, over-focusing on the children, using drugs, or working more at the office. Sometimes this works like a thermostat within a relationship—when the temperature gets too hot the thermostat kicks on the "air conditioner" to cool things off, or if it is too cool, the heat get turned up. We all can think of ways we know how to "cool things off" or "heat things up" in our relationships.

One strategy used to attempt to keep the temperature in the relationship stable is by telling a lie and keeping secrets about the lie. For every lie that is told, another is told to cover the first one. Sometimes silence (lying by omission) is the lie. It doesn't take a rocket scientist to know that when one is spending significant amounts of time thinking about the lie, making up the lie, presenting the lie, making up another falsehood to secure the first one, worrying about whether there is evidence somewhere that will expose the lie, creating evidence to further cover the lie, acting some way to further secure the lie, reviewing the story with someone else asked to hold onto the lie, wondering if you need to bribe that person to keep the lie, and wondering if you need to buy your partner something so she won't suspect the deception—there is not much time or energy left for anything else. You can see how secrets and lies can shape the behavior in a relationship.

Most people think addicts lie more than partners or that addicts lie to everybody and partners only fool themselves. Examine below the reasons why addicts lie and see what you think. Can you think of other reasons why you have lied?

Why Addicts Lie

Although most addicts lie to cover their tracks, the real fear is that if the partner knew the truth, there would be no way for her to forgive him. The addict fears the partner will leave. That fear of loss motivates the addict to lie more than anything.

Addicts are famous for lies of omission. Do you recognize this situation? Your partner senses something is up. You don't want to lie, so if she doesn't ask you specifically, you do not offer the information. Or perhaps you are worried that telling her the truth will hurt her so much, you can't possibly do it, and so you deliberately leave out the most troubling part of what happened. Mostly, you don't want to further incriminate yourself! Perhaps you have been caught and are scared, but your partner does not know everything about what you have done. You tell part of the truth to reduce your guilt and to be able to say that you told the truth, but you fail to give your partner a valuable piece of information that will help her make a decision about her future.

But addicts also lie for different reasons. Here are the ones mentioned most often in our research.

Withdrawal is Scary and Painful

Withdrawal from any drug (even the chemicals that the brain makes for the pornography or gambling addict) is painful and scary. Once the addict is entrenched in the addiction cycle, the brain continues to crave the neurotransmitter changes the addictive cycle has created. Stopping addictive behavior results in urges, cravings, and often in unpleasant or painful withdrawal symptoms. Many addicts have no clue what to do to get the brain to stop calling out for more drugs. The addictive behavior has also been a reliable source of companionship, emotional pain relief, and glue that has held the addict together. Giving that up is frightening and emotionally painful, even when the addict is highly motivated to stop using.

Keeping the Mask Firmly Attached

All addicts portray an image that they think others want to see. To tell the truth means letting go of that safe identity. The real fear is that if your partner knew what you were really like, your partner would leave you.

Fear of Loss

Loss of control: If I lose control something bad will happen to me. If I don't have control then you do. You already run my life; it would be impossible for me if you controlled it even more. I don't want to be dominated (engulfed/smothered).

Loss of opportunity: If you know, then how will I tolerate this pain without my "fix"?

Loss of children: If you know, will you take my children or turn them against me?

Loss of finances: Will you punish me by taking everything I have worked for all my life?

Loss of home: Will you kick me out and where will I go?

Loss of image: Will you tell our friends and then I will have no one on my side?

The fear of real and imagined losses seems never ending.

Fear of Emotions

Addicts report these thoughts: "If I tell you, the consequences will be too painful." "I can't stand conflict. I don't know what to say when you confront me or when you are that angry. It reminds me too much of when my mom/dad got angry and I did not have an answer then either." "I can't tolerate the pain of the past or what I think the future will bring." "I do care about her and I don't want to see my partner hurt. Any way I do this, it will just kill her. She just can't take it."

Denial

Most addicts have thought, "If I pretend that all is well, then I don't have to face the fact that I'm screwed up and have made this relationship a disaster." Denial is one of those things that helps you or hurts you. Denial is a necessary part of grieving, protecting you from pain for a while. However, if you never face the pain, it gets worse and becomes the source of more trouble. To be in denial is to say that you don't have a problem or that you don't have to face the consequences of your behavior. Eventually you do—life becomes an out-of-control mess. To avoid the reality of your life is to avoid taking responsibility for your life. The only way to get better is to be accountable for your life, take responsibility, and move through the pain.

Disclosing a secret sometimes leads to favorable results, but sometimes telling results in devastating consequences. Finding out someone is keeping secrets throws the relationship into turmoil. Either way, the process of creating, keeping, telling, and hearing the secret alters the relationship in very important ways.

Many addicts say they lie and resist disclosure because they don't want to hurt their partner. That stance shows little respect for your partner. Our research shows that over 90% of partners wanted to be told the truth because they were made to feel crazy—as if the reality they were seeing did not exist. Despite the pain, they felt better about being told. The next chapter discusses the consequences of telling, the good, bad and ugly.

Chapter Three

Is Disclosure Right for You?
If, When, and How Much To Tell

Disclosures come in all forms; some are done with integrity and some are done in the worst way possible. Obviously, if you are reading this book you are considering disclosure, have disclosed to someone, and are looking for ways to make things easier and better.

It is safe to say that all revelations are painful for everyone, often initially traumatic for the partner, and hard for the couple. Yet, most partners and addicts (over 90% in our study) report they are glad the disclosure happened. This high approval and the fact that most couples did not split up after disclosure (see Chapter 4) led us to think that the couples who had acknowledged the secrets had a better chance of saving the relationship than those who had not.

When the disclosure is done with integrity, both the addict and partner may experience a kind of relief. The partner may experience a wide variety of other feelings, but also often feels validated because her suspicions were correct and she isn't crazy. The addict feels a sense of freedom from the secret life and relief from the shame. This relief is immediate for some; for others it takes more time. But the reduction of anxiety and stress allows a period of time during which the couple can begin to examine the impact of the addiction on both their lives.

The primary core of healing is forgiveness, but true forgiveness can never happen unless the truth is known. When the secret or lie remains undisclosed, it festers and grows into a bigger wound. But who you tell, when you tell, what you tell, and how you tell are the keys to a successful, healing disclosure.

Forgiveness

If you want to stop living a lie, and have your relationship survive and grow, then your partner has to know about your problem. Awareness of your difficulty also gives your partner a better chance of identifying and dealing with her own problems. Other people who need to know may include your children, other family members, select people at work, or best friends. Revealing your secrets to these people is different in many ways than disclosing to your partner. This issue is discussed in sections of Chapters 6 through 8.

Several things impact how well a couple does after disclosure–the type of betrayal, each person's attachment style (anxious, avoidant, or secure) and emotional competence skill level, if there have been repeated relapses, and types of unresolved issues between the couple. The commitment each person has to working on their own health and as well as the relationship health varies depending on the context of each person's life. Couples also do better when they are committed to common goals such as improving communication, co-parenting in ways that honor and protect their children, allowing each to experience feelings without returning to old ways of relating, making and accepting agreed upon restitution, and eventually moving towards rather than away from each other. This is not easy; often people are so beaten down by the unhealthy relationship that staying stuck in anger and fear seems easier than working on self- improvement or relationship skills, especially forgiveness. Certainly at the point of disclosure, the addict has made decisions about moving forward, but for the partner, disclosure often throws her back into fear and anger and it is very difficult for her to know what she wants. The partner's level of emotional response is frequently a trigger for the addict, so careful planning for relapse prevention and support for both is important.

Fortunately, with time and work towards awareness, the anger and fear do lessen, recovery gets under way and clarity about goals and decisions for the future can be made. While some level of forgiveness is essential for peace of mind and healing, it takes time and requires much of both people in the relationship. Forgiveness may be an important part of the couple's healing work; forgiving oneself is essential for the individual to heal. Because disclosure is often the first step toward forgiveness, we want to digress here and summarize the steps to forgiveness.

According to Karl Tomm, M.D. of the University of Calgary, there are two contrasting methods in which a person restores a sense of self-worth after being hurt. The first, often initially used by the partner, is to diminish the worth of the other through retaliation or revenge, striking out in anger and fear. The second is to enhance self-worth through competence and forgiveness. We believe the second method is by far the better and healthier way to restore self-worth. Being able to manage your emotions is a must, but forgiveness is what enables a person to manage resentment and anger in the wake of being wronged. This is very difficult for partners, so do not ask for forgiveness at disclosure. To do so shows you are insensitive to the aftershock of hearing about your betrayals. You might hope for forgiveness, but your partner will have to go through a process to get to where she/he wants or is able to forgive.

Even though we are discussing forgiveness early in the book, it does not really happen until the partner has chance to understand the impact your behavior has had on her/his life and when there has been an ample amount of evidence your intention to change is proven through your behavior. Your behavior has been a form of abuse – to your partner and to yourself. Steps that lead to forgiveness reflect those seen in recovery from any trauma and it takes time. In her book, *The Unburdened Heart*, Mariah Burton-Nelson, a famous sports journalist, wrote about her healing journey years after having been molested by her high school coach. Burton-Nelson describes the first stage of healing as awareness that a wrong has been done and it has had a huge impact on her life. She is quick to point out that the first defense against the pain that comes with this awareness is denial. Denial is a close personal friend of every addict and most partners. The addicted person uses denial to convince himself that he won't get caught, that the behavior isn't so bad, or that this will be the last time he acts out. Likewise the partner uses denial to brush aside the evidence that something is going on, and that things will get better if she just tries harder. But without the awareness of what happened and how it affected everyone involved, it is difficult to know what impact it had on you and others and what needs to be forgiven. The disclosure process allows clarity and validation of what happened and who was responsible for what. It is through these first events of talking, listen-ing, and validating experiences that healing can begin. Disclosure can bring an end to denial and thus a beginning to forgiveness.

During this time you will be wise to keep in mind what the late author and researcher Dr. Shirley Glass says in her excellent book, *Not Just Friends*. First and foremost – forgiveness is for YOUR PARTNER not for you. It won't take away your fear or take away the betrayal of what has happened.

In her book, *How Can I Forgive You? The Courage to Forgive, the Freedom Not To,* Janis Abrahms Spring describes four approaches to forgiveness. The first two are dysfunctional: Cheap forgiveness is a quick desperate attempt to preserve the relationship even if you ignore your partner's pain. It is premature, superficial, and undeserved. It is offered before your partner processes the impact of your behavior, asks anything of you, or thinks about what lies ahead. Refusal to forgive is the approach your partner might take when he or she wants to pun-ish an unremorseful mate, when your partner believes she can forgive only if she is ready to reconcile or have compassion for you which she does not feel, or if your partner believes that forgiveness is a sign of weakness.

In contrast, there are two types of forgiveness which are adaptive and useful: Acceptance is a healthy response to a hurt when the addict can't or won't engage in the healing process. It asks nothing of the offender, but rather is a program of self-care for your partner, part of which is to stop "giving you free rent in her head," as members of 12-step programs say. Spring calls it "clearing your head of emotional poison." Instead, your partner lets go of revenge fantasies, ensures her emotional and physical safety, and creates a relationship with you that satisfies her own goals, including getting along with you if that's in her best interest. She may or may not choose to have any further relationship with you. And she accepts that you may never change.

Finally, genuine forgiveness is what can happen when you participate in the healing process. According to Spring, you must earn genuine forgiveness, while your partner allows you to settle your debt. She writes, "As he works hard to earn forgiveness through genuine, generous acts of repentance and restitution, the hurt party works hard to let go of her resentments and need for retribution. If either of you fails to do the requisite work, there can be no Genuine Forgiveness."

Forgiving is not forgetting or pretending that it did not happen or that the behavior wasn't such a big deal. It was and *is* a big deal for your partner. By forgiving someone the hurtful act, a person does not forget what happened. Forgiving is also not excusing. Excusing is appropriate when you believe the person was not to blame for the wrongdoing; your partner may forgive because she/he is ready to let go of the pain that binds her/him to the memory. Forgiving is also not condoning or tolerating. Your partner can forgive you without condoning what you did. Your partner may set firmer boundaries and seek support from others as a way to protect herself. Most likely, your partner will not be willing to tolerate similar actions in the future. And ultimately, your partner also may forgive you yet realize she/he cannot have you in her/his life. Taking responsibility for your behavior and the impact it has and will continue to have on your partner will help your partner see your accountability – a behavior that helps clarify your intention to change.

As the addict, it will be useful for you to list all the people you have hurt with your addiction and the various ways you have hurt them. This is what the Eighth Step of AA is about. Be sure to include yourself in the list, as your actions have certainly harmed you too Realize the ways you used denial to help you stay detached from the feelings you experience from hurting those people on the list. When you are ready to make a formal amends, acknowledging how you used denial and the hurtful impact your behavior has had on your partner and others will help your partner see that you have a sense of what she or he experienced during that time. That will help her/him move towards forgiveness but it takes time.

When to Tell

Jeff, who'd been actively involved in addiction recovery for six months, desperately wanted his wife Jody to participate with him in recovery activities. He saw some of his program friends being supported emotionally by their spouses, speaking the language of recovery together, being able to let go of the shameful secrets they'd been keeping. But John was afraid to tell Jody about his past addictive activities that he'd managed to keep secret for so long.

Finally he saw what seemed the perfect opportunity—a weekend workshop for couples recovering from addiction. He signed himself and Jody up, telling her it was a marriage enrichment program. During the two-hour drive to the retreat center where the program was to be held, Jeff told his wife about the hundreds of lies he had fed her, the hours he had spent at the race track drinking and gambling, the hours spent on the computer at night when she thought he was asleep, the online risks he had taken, as well as about the young woman he met at the dog track who had offered him a blow-job for $20 after he had won. As he drove, he began crying as he told her what happened next: While he was in the restroom stall with his pants down around his ankles—never thinking he could ever do something like that – this woman stole the money he had won and the remainder of his pay-check. Jeff hoped that over the weekend she would have help from the other couples and the facilitators in processing the disclosure, so he told her about everything he'd done.

When the couple arrived at the retreat center, Jody was trau-matized, in a state of shock. The two facilitators found themselves unexpectedly faced with a woman in crisis, in need of immediate one-on-one attention. Leaving the first group session to his associate, one of the facilitators ended up spending the entire evening counseling and supporting Jody. The following morning she was able to join the group and explain what had happened.

Jeff had good intentions—to disclose to Jody in a setting where she would have support. But the manner in which he chose to do this was unfair to Jody and put an additional burden on the weekend facilitators, who had not planned for, and did not have the man-power for, one-on-one crisis counseling. Plus Jody was in an impos-sible situation—reeling from the shock and the shame and self-blame that often results from the disclosure of infidelity, she was not yet ready to have 30 other people immediately hear about her situ-ation. Given that Jeff had the opportunity for a planned disclosure, it would have been better for him to arrange with his therapist to bring Jody into therapy, assess her emotional state, and disclose to her in therapy.

Sara and Sam had been married three years when Sam started attending Twelve-step meetings for cocaine addiction. Sam had not mentioned to Sara that he was also addicted to sex and frequently sought out sexual encounters with prostitutes while using cocaine. During the Twelve-step meetings, his sponsor and other group members encouraged Sam to tell Sara about the sexual encounters because she may have been exposed to a sexually transmitted disease as a result of his behavior. Sam feared that disclosure would mean the loss of his marriage and his son.

On more than one occasion Sam had had sex with Sara after having had unprotected sex with a prostitute when he was high. In fact, he had admitted to his sponsor that at times he had been so unaware of reality when he was using, that it simply had not occurred to him to use a condom. His love for Sarah motivated Sam to disclose to her because he realized she needed to know that he might have exposed her to an STD, even HIV. Sam was determined to disclose but did not know how. His sponsor suggested that Sam tell his wife in the presence of the sponsor, a therapist, or perhaps the minister from his church. However, Sam was so consumed with shame and anxiety that he called Sara right after the Twelve-step meeting. In the midst of panic and shame he told her,

> *"Sara, I've been at my CA meeting and the guys tell me I really need to tell you that I, ah, ah, once, when I was really out of it using crack, I hired a prostitute and had sex with her. I don't remember if I used a rubber or not, so you should go get tested for AIDS right away." He was crying now and quickly rambled, "I'm sorry; I know you are really mad now, but please don't leave me or take Ryan. I love you both and can't live without you. I'd kill myself if you left me. Please tell me you won't leave. I'll do anything to make this up to you. Please, please, you are more important to me than anything."*

Sara was stunned by what she heard. In shock she thought, "What does he mean? First the crack cocaine, now this! And an AIDS test! What is happening? What is wrong with me that he would have to have sex with a prostitute? When did this happen? My God, what am I going to do?" The fact that Sam told her over the phone just made her confusion worse. She said, "I don't understand? What do you mean prostitute?" Then she began to scream and cry at the same time, "AIDS! How could you do this to me? Don't you love me? Was it because I wouldn't let you have anal sex with me? You told me you just had a little problem with cocaine and now you say crack! Are you really on meth? Or is it heroin? Why didn't you tell me before? Why would you lie to me like this? How could you do this to me?" As she began to sob, she slammed down the phone.

In the ideal world, disclosure takes place in the therapist's office, after the addict and partner have both been prepared in earlier therapy sessions to go through the initial stages of this process and have been advised how much to ask and how much to reveal. In Chapter 5, we will describe a formal disclosure from start to finish.

In reality, the first disclosure often happens precipitously when someone actually gets caught red-handed. For example, a woman may walk in on her husband when he has just snorted a line of cocaine or perhaps when he's masturbating while "chatting" with someone online or looking at pornography, and demand an explanation. A man may observe his wife taking money from her mother's purse while her mother is in the restroom during dinner in a restaurant. Seeing a huge increase in the cost of automobile insurance due to a ticket for driving under the influence of alcohol may elicit questions from a partner. A man may have his credit card denied only to find when he gets home that his wife is in front of the computer, gambling online and that their bank account is overdrawn and savings depleted. A man is arrested for possession of methamphetamines while soliciting a prostitute who happens to be an undercover police officer, and he calls his wife from jail. Such situations demand immediate disclosure. Typically, the person on the spot will attempt "damage control" by revealing as little as possible, most often only what he thinks the partner already knows or is likely to find out.

Another type of precipitous disclosure occurs when the person holding the secret comes to believe he can no longer live with it, and dumps everything on an unprepared and unsuspecting partner, as happened to Jody and Sara in the vignette above. To make matters worse, the disclosure may happen over the phone or in an email or text message, rather than in person.

For example, Daniel, a physician who had had sexual relations with several patients, was admitted to a treatment center in another state. After a few days there he phoned his wife Lorelei. She reported,

> *Daniel didn't have the guts to tell me face to face, so he told me over the phone. He was safely away at the treatment center surrounded by nurturing caring professionals and fellow addicts. I was in our bedroom painting furniture, surrounded by our five small children. Laundry needed to be done; dishes from supper were waiting on me. I had to talk to him as though nothing was happening to my heart. It was horrible! I felt so alone and desperate! But what could I do?*

Lorelei continued,

> *I never would have believed for a minute he would actually have sex with anyone outside our marriage. I would actually have bet money on it. I was absolutely shocked by the seriousness and extent of his addictions and the many years he'd been lying to me. There never would have been an easy way to disclose all this stuff, but I deserved better. He described all the times he'd had sex with other people, and then said he did it because I was too tired all the time to have sex. He just went on and on. I didn't even hear half of it. I was in so much shock. I should have been given the same supportive environment as my husband, surrounded by other people in my circumstances. If I had not had those kids to take care of, I'm not sure what I would have done to myself.*

Years later, Lorelei still harbors resentment over the way this disclosure was carried out. This contaminated her ability to separate her anger at the acting out behaviors from her anger at the insensitivity of the disclosure and she admits that there is a part of her that never allows herself to trust him or be vulnerable again. Despite lots of work, she reports that his behavior has irreparably damaged the relationship.

Unexpected disclosures via letters or email are just as damaging as phone calls. Georgia, a bright young attorney, shared her story with us:

> *My husband left me a letter on what I call "the morning from hell." I was in a hurry when I left the house because I was on my way to my doctor's office to confirm a recent home pregnancy test I had taken. I just picked up that letter and stuck it in my purse and off I went,*

anticipating, thinking about maybe being pregnant. I forgot about the letter until I opened my purse to get in the car. Reading that letter, alone, in the car in the parking lot after leaving the doctor's office, was devastating. Here I was, just having received information that I was pregnant! This should have been the happiest day of my life—instead I was shocked beyond belief. But I had so much shame about what he said he had done, I couldn't tell anyone. I was dazed. I truly believe God drove the car the 10 miles home because I didn't even see the road. I felt suicidal—even pictured killing him and then myself. I never thought myself capable of considering those actions. I felt betrayed by the person I trusted the most. I went into shock. I was numb. I lost the baby eight weeks later and to be honest, even today I still blame him.

Television talk and reality shows are yet another venue for inappropriate disclosures of secrets, sometimes with devastating consequences. In a highly publicized case, host Jenny Jones, in a program taped in March 1995, had a 26-year-old guest, Jonathan Schmitz, who was told only that he had a secret admirer. The secret admirer turned out to be a young gay man, Scott Amedure. The surprised Schmitz, who reportedly had a psychiatric history, was so distressed at being the public object of a homosexual crush that days later he shot Amedure dead. Schmitz was eventually sentenced to 25–50 years in prison for second-degree murder. Jenny Jones was subsequently sued successfully for her role in this murder.

The opening scene from an older movie *Hope Floats* is another good example of how not to do a disclosure. The heroine, Birdee Calvert, is invited to be a guest on a popular afternoon talk show where her best friend is going to share a "secret" with her. Birdie thinks this is just a funny gag and goes along. What her best friend tells her is that she (the best friend) is having an affair with Birdee's husband Bill. Birdee is naturally devastated as her whole life falls apart.

Electronic media has become a place for inappropriate disclosure in many ways. From sending sexually explicit photos texts or emails, to revealing information that was meant to be private, these types of disclosures often lead to disastrous endings. A tragic ending happened in September 2010, when a 19 year old student at Rutgers University, Tyler Clementi, was secretly videotaped kissing a man with a webcam set up by his roommate, Dharun Ravi while Molly Wei, a fellow dorm mate viewed the encounter in her dorm room. A couple of days later, Ravi encouraged friends and Twitter followers to watch Clementi in a second encounter with his male friend thereby disclosing (without Tyler's permission) that Tyler was gay and engaging in romantic encounters with men. Even though the viewing never occurred, Tyler was alerted of the Twitter message and the following day, Tyler tragically ended his life by jumping from the George Washington Bridge. Ravi and Wei were indicted for their roles in the webcam incident. This type of disclosure also constitutes cyberbullying. Electronic media is not the place to disclose. Information which is meant for one person and to remain private can easily be electronically shared with anyone with access to the Internet.

There is a right and a wrong way to handle disclosures that result from suspicions or from incriminating evidence and revelations that are a complete surprise to the partner. Later in this chapter we will make recommendations regarding the timing and content of these disclosures.

You might consider if you have postponed telling your partner because you are concerned over her or his welfare. What conditions do you think need to change in order for you to be ready to tell? What will be evidence that the time is right? How might you be making things worse?

How Much to Tell

Unfortunately, most addicts' first attempts at disclosure come when incriminating evidence is discovered and then the addict tells only what he thinks will generate the least painful immediate consequences. Children learn early on to lie to avoid pain, and, until people get pretty healthy, they continue to repeat this behavior as adults. For addicts, it is a way of life.

In our studies of sex addicts and partners who had experienced disclosure, addicts reported that coming clean brought relief, ended denial, and proved to be the gateway to recovery for the individual and the relationship. But it was not all positive. Disclosure also brought shame to the addict, pain to the partner, and fears about loss of the relationship for both.

Some addicts had revealed every single detail of their sexual acting out, and they suffered negative consequences for it. Several wished they had disclosed differently. This was particularly true for addicts in early recovery. For example, Clark, 28, who'd been in recovery for 10 months, wrote,

> *I feel I offered too much information. To admit I was involved with another woman was one thing, but I truly wish I had never told her who the woman was. She became obsessed with trying to find this woman and search for proof that I was still seeing her. Some people cannot handle truth and honesty as well as others. You have to know your partner and what they can handle.*

Eleven months after his disclosure, Ben, 31, related,

> *I hope it wasn't just "dumping," but I felt cleaner, relieved. But I shouldn't have shared so much, it was hurtful to her. Now it's hard for her to have so much information. The knowledge doesn't help her and seems only to cause pain as dates roll around or if we drive past a particular place. She can't stop thinking about it."*

After living with an addicted person, it is natural for a partner to easily become obsessed with his behaviors. If that obsession becomes intrusive for the partner—she literally can't stop thinking about it months or even years after the disclosure—she is having symptoms of post-traumatic stress and may need professional help. The obsession is a sign that the disclosure has gone awry.

Partners often begin by demanding complete honesty, which is a way for them to make sense of the past, to validate their suspicions and the reality they had experienced which had often been denied by the addict. Partners long to have a sense of control of the situation, to assess their risk of having been exposed to financial disaster, violence, and diseases. They want to evaluate the commitment of their partner to the future of the relationship. One partner said, "If I didn't get information, I could not trust the relationship to go forward. I needed every question answered, or I would not have been able to trust and therefore stay in the marriage. I can deal with truths, but not half-truths."

However, sometimes things get worse before they get better. Disclosure often creates more problems than you think it will. When a disclosure happens the partner may also spontaneously reveal her own set of secrets. This creates one more layer of work that has to be handled by the couple and by each individual.

Finding out that someone has been arrested and can anticipate legal consequences will affect the family for decades because of reporting requirements, probation, and loss of financial assets. In some cases the existence of another family creates ripples that members of both families will feel for years to come. One can never be 100% sure where disclosure will lead. Nonetheless, both addicts and partners have learned that honesty is the best way to find healing.

Reveal All Now, or Save the Worst for Later: The Pain of Staggered Disclosure

As the country witnessed in 1998, President Clinton's first disclosures were denials, when he repeatedly stated, "I did not have sexual relations with that woman, Ms. Lewinsky." Subsequent acknowledgments were of limited information. However, President Clinton's process of disclosure seemed to have made the situation worse for himself and his family. Despite the nation watching these staggered revelations, we have witnessed numerous public figures deny any wrong doing in the beginning, only to confess the truth later on. More recently the marriage of former California Governor Arnold Schwartzenegger ended after national news broke the story that he'd had a child with his long-term housekeeper. These are powerful demonstrations that staggered disclosure usually doesn't work for long and makes everyone angrier and less trustful. Many wives forgive their husbands after learning of an affair. But if they later learn that the husband continued to keep secrets for years while maintaining some type of relationship with an employee with whom he had daily contact, or a prostitute to whom he paid many thousands of dollars, it may become too painful to forgive.

Disclosure is painful, and often precipitates a crisis in the couple's relationship. It is hard enough for someone to admit to being a drug addict, or gambling away a family's livelihood, or having food control one's life. But disclosure is even harder for sex addicts or addicts who have both a drug and sexual addiction, often with a long list of secret sexual activities in which they have engaged. This is made even worse by an equally long list of lies that were told to cover up the activities.

When considering the consequences of the disclosure, addicts fear that the partner will leave them. Our research showed that the majority of partners do threaten to leave should they learn of an affair (in our original research, 60% of partners threatened to leave but less than one quarter of that group left). This is often the case for other types of addicts too—the partner threatens to leave if the addict doesn't stop the behavior. Female addicts in particular may fear physical or sexual violence from their partners as a response to the revelations. Both male and female addicts may worry that an angry spouse will use the information against them as a means of emotional blackmail or in a future battle for custody of the children.

It is tempting for an addict to attempt damage control by initially revealing only some of what he or she did. Often, only the least damaging information is admitted, or else only those activities that the person believes their partner already knows about. Then, at some future time, the addict discloses additional secrets, or the partner learns the whole truth independently. Unfortunately, this strategy turns out to be very short-sighted, and likely to increase the chances of an unfavorable outcome in the long run.

In our survey, 59% of addicts and 70% of partners reported that there had been more than one major disclosure. This was not always because the addict had deliberately withheld information. Some addicts did not initially remember all their actions, especially if their addictions included multiple episodes or different types of activities or drugs. In other cases, it was only after experiencing some time in recovery that the addict realized that certain behaviors were sufficiently important that they should have been divulged. The lesson here is that *disclosure is more likely to be a process than a one-time event.* Whatever the reason for the staggered disclosures, the process is particularly difficult for the person at the receiving end. It is especially destructive when the reason was a deliberate lie.

A recurrent theme among partners is the damage of staggered disclosure by the addict. When the addict claims at the time to reveal all the relevant facts but actually withheld the most difficult information for later admission, partners reported greater difficulty in restoring trust. One woman wrote:

There were several major disclosures over six months. I was completely devastated. He continued to disclose half-truths—but only when his lies didn't make sense so that he was backed to the wall. This only increased my pain and anger and made the whole situation worse. Each new disclosure was like reliving the initial pain all over again. Part of that was not being told. I felt lied to and didn't trust any of the relationship. All I wanted was the truth. I wish the truth had been admitted all at once and not in bits and pieces.

Another woman wrote of her feelings after her husband lost his job because of his sexual misconduct:

He had to tell me something because he was fired, and people in his profession are seldom fired for any reason other than gross malpractice or sexual misconduct. He told me he had sexually touched a subordinate at work. He said it was invited, which turned out not to be true. His revelations continued to dribble out over weeks as I continued to ask for information. Each new piece of information felt like a scab being ripped off.

A similar strategy, with tragic results, was used by a physician who had sex with several patients and was asked to appear before his licensing board. Initially, he told his wife that a single patient had complained to the board; that it was all a misunderstanding. Convinced of his innocence, his wife insisted on accompanying him to the hearing to support him. It turned out that several of his victims were present and told their stories, in a very credible manner. What she heard was a litany of behaviors that shocked and stunned not only the Board, but also the local press that was in attendance. The wife said she didn't care about the other allegations, just the last one. She asked her husband if he'd had sex with that woman. At that point he felt he had to tell her the truth. He later recalled,

I will never forget the look that came across her face. It was the look of ultimate pain that comes with betrayal, a shattered dream, a broken promise, and a broken heart. She walked out of the room and out of my life, never again to love me as a wife. I'd lost not only my career, but also my wife and daughter.

Sexually exploitative professionals and other public figures often initially try to minimize their misconduct, not only to licensing boards and assessment teams, but also to their spouses. When a wife who has publicly supported her husband because she believed in his innocence eventually learns that he continued to lie to her about the allegations after they were made public, her public humiliation and sense of betrayal are compounded, and the healing is that much more difficult.

The addict may be so frightened that what he or she has disclosed may truly be all they were capable of at the time. For example, Sam had revealed his worst behavior, but had kept to himself some other forms of sexual acting out in which he had indulged. When Sam heard that staggered disclosure is to be avoided in favor of full disclosure of all the elements of a person's sexual acting out, his eyes filled with tears and he told his therapy group,

> *I was so scared to tell my wife about my voyeurism, I could barely manage to get through it. I thought I would die right there! There's no way I could possibly have told her about the other stuff. You have to realize that sometimes a partial disclosure is all you can do!*

Sam's point is well taken: A partial disclosure is better than no disclosure at all, and sometimes it takes all the courage an addict has to explain to his partner some of what he has done. The spouse who later gets upset at hearing additional information may find it helpful to recognize that the addict may have been doing his best at the time.

One of the most important things we have learned from talking with partners of sex addicts is that staggered disclosures are very destructive to the relationship. The spouse may spend weeks or months after the initial disclosure learning to trust again, only to have the rug pulled out from beneath her or him by learning of additional secrets and lies that had not previously been revealed. In fact, often new lies had been generated to cover up the old ones, such as "I've told you everything," or "This time I'm telling you the truth." It is our belief that what is most helpful for the restoration of the relationship is for addicts initially to disclose at least the broad outlines of all their significant compulsive activities, rather than holding back some damaging material.

To summarize, because early on, the partner tends to want to know "everything," sometimes with negative consequences, we recommend that the partner discuss with a counselor or therapist what details are really important to know and what the likely effect will be on the partner.

Nonetheless, there are several circumstances when delayed disclosure is inevitable. This is why you and your partner need to understand that *disclosure is a process*, not a one-time event. Some situations are:

- The addict has acted out in so many different ways or with so many different people, or has told so many lies, that he or she genuinely does not recall some of them until a later time.

- The addict was in such an altered state at the time of the some of the episodes of acting out—especially when associated with drinking or drug use—that he simply does not remember particular events.

- The addict, although remembering all the details of his acting out, does not initially consider particular events or actions significant enough to bother disclosing. With increased recovery, the addict realizes the need for disclosing additional history.

- Revelation of certain actions may be so damaging to the partner or to family relations (for example, an affair with the wife's sister, purchasing and using drugs with a brother who is a minor, driving under the influence of alcohol or other drugs with children in the car), or may entail significant risk of violence to the addict (for example, a female addict married to a man who has a history of physically abusing her), that a therapist recommends not disclosing these facts initially, until the partner or family member has received counseling and preparation.

- Certain episodes of acting out occurred only after the initial disclosure. That is, they represented slips or relapses of the addiction. (This is the most problematic situation, in that it is likely to cause the most damage to the process of rebuilding trust.)

The take-home message is that following the first disclosure it is important to make a plan of how to manage further revelations if the addicted person later remembers more information or realizes something important has been left out.

Should I Tell "All the Gory Details"?

In our survey, disclosure of various details often turned out to be "devastating" and "traumatic" and left recipients with unpleasant memories and associations that were difficult to ignore. Lara, who persuaded her husband to tell her "everything," regretted it:

> I created a lot of pain for myself by asking questions about details and gathering information. I have a lot of negative memories to overcome; this ranges from songs on the radio to dates, places, and situations; there are numerous triggers.

In later recovery, partners typically reported that they recognized that knowledge is not necessarily power, that no matter how much information they had they were still unable to control the addict. Instead, they developed guidelines for themselves about what information they wanted (typically more general information such as health risks, financial consequences affecting them, and level of commitment to recovery and the relationship) and what they did not want (such as details of what the high was like, sexual activities, locations, and numbers of partners).

Another partner spoke about the difficulty of hearing all the details.

> I think it's best for the addict to work through it with a knowledgeable therapist, then disclose the nature of the problem and have the partner determine what level of detail they are comfortable with. For me, I didn't want any more detail, because it tormented me. Others feel they want to know everything Not me. The bottom line I needed to know was whether he was exposing himself to disease, and then not protecting me. The actual details of who, where, and when were extremely distracting to me and caused me to lose ground. I'd make some progress, then think about one of those details and spiral down.

It can be very helpful for partners to have a therapist encourage them to consider carefully what information they seek rather than ask for "everything."

Private Information vs. Secret Information

In the recovering community "rigorous honesty" is virtually a dogma, and people get the idea that if you keep any kind of information from your partner you are lying and thus on the verge of a relapse. Any omission becomes the catalyst for suspicion and recriminations. It is important to separate out what information is private and what is secret:

Anita had been involved with several men over the past year. Alcohol, cocaine, and having sex with men at conferences had been part of her ritual for many years. Yet when she found out she was pregnant, she knew she had to stop if she had any hope of sanity for herself or her marriage. Because her husband had had a vasectomy, she knew that the pregnancy could not possibly be his, and because of potential problems with the fetus due to her drug use, she opted to have an abortion. When she was preparing her disclosure with her therapist, she said, "I'm so confused about what to do. My peers in SLAA tell me that I am keeping secrets and harming my recovery, but I just don't think it will help our situation for me to tell him about this abortion. It was a private decision between me and my God, and not a part of our relationship. Still, I don't even know who the father was! I just don't want to screw up my recovery. Should I tell?"

In this case, Anita has done well to evaluate how it might help or further complicate the situation to tell her husband. She is correct that the decision legally is hers to make and is a private matter. If she is convinced that telling would help her stay sober, she can decide to tell information that is private. Had her husband been the father, although the decision remains hers legally, he would have had the right to know so he could at least voice his opinion, allowing him to grieve the loss and/or support her in the decision, and to experience any emotions that might arise about the pregnancy and drug use. Either way, she is faced with the consequences of her decision.

How about the case of Marty, married to Suzy, who had gotten Sandy, his secretary, pregnant during a two-year affair with her. Would he be keeping a secret if he did not tell Suzy that Sandy reported having an abortion shortly after the affair ended? Is it a secret or private? Would it be different if Suzy and Marty had been trying to get pregnant for several years with no success?

In this case, Suzy had a right to know because Marty's actions could result in legal consequences (sexual harassment) since Sandy was an employee. Also, she might still be pregnant and waiting until a later date to sue him for child support and medical care. This would directly impact Suzy. To make matters worse, Sandy's best friend, who ran the local newspaper, saw Marty come out of the Motel 6 with Sandy and photographed them together. No amount of back-pedaling on Marty's part could save him from Suzy if the story about a sexual harassment suit showed up in bold print on the front page of the local paper. In order for Suzy to make decisions about staying, boundary setting, what to do if the media got involved, and what to tell the children and family members, Marty would be wise to disclose before someone else does.

It is sometimes hard to know what is private and what is a secret. What is private does not interfere with someone else's physical or emotional health or cut us off from the resources we need to solve problems. A secret prevents one person (or both) from making truly informed decisions.

Secrets sometimes become private information once they are shared with the appropriate people. So it is important to decide who else needs to know the information. It is not appropriate for the addict to tell everyone his First Step or for the spouse to tell all her friends and relatives specific information contained in a disclosure. Decide who needs to know before making the private moment between you and your spouse a public display of pain without boundaries–that is one good reason to do disclosure with a therapist who knows something about addiction and lots about couples.

Interim Disclosure

We recommend a planned, thoughtful, full disclosure as early as possible. In cases where you as an addicted person are not prepared for a full disclosure, but you know it's quite likely your partner will find out about some of your addictive behavior, then an interim disclosure is in order. This means revealing information that you know your partner will find out anyway. Be prepared that your partner may not accept the interim and press you for more detail. Have a set time in which you will strive to have your formal disclosure ready and set an appointment with her for that time and date.

Tell your partner that you are preparing an amends letter that includes more specific information and at that reading you will answer any questions she may have about your behavior. Invite her to start a list of questions and her own letter about how this makes her feel. Acknowledge her frustration over not getting everything today, and admit you are telling her this because you want her to hear it from you rather than someone else. Request that she talk with a therapist or someone she trusts about how she is feeling. Indicate that you are sorry for the behavior you have engaged in and will keep her posted about what you are doing for your recovery. Assure her that you are committed to the relationship and that you are sorry for the harm you have caused. Stay sober, and keep your appointment with her.

The Therapist and Secret-Keeping

Whether or not to disclose a secret is a decision for the therapist as well as the client. The therapist's decision can significantly impact the effectiveness of the therapy. Some therapists continue working with the couple while holding the secret, hoping that they can still assist the couple to improve their relationship. Other therapists insist that secrets be shared and will refer you to someone else if you choose not to disclose. If you are seeking a counselor or therapist to work on relationship as well as addiction problems that include secrets, ask the therapist about his or her training and experiences. Also ask the therapist about his or her experience with addiction and the policy for insisting on disclosure if he or she sees the clients individually. How will this affect your ability to maintain recovery or trust the therapist? This should help you decide if this therapist is right for you.

The final chapter in this book is for therapists. If you have a good relationship with a therapist, you probably want to stay with him or her. You may want to share this chapter with your therapist.

Suggestions for Addicts Regarding Disclosure

Obviously, not all partners are in an emotionally safe place to hear a disclosure—but most can handle it if you have been thoughtful about the disclosure. Not all partners want to hear it all. But for your partner's sake and your own do not leave a letter, send an email, or make a phone call—have the integrity to tell in person what you have done after doing adequate preparation.

Sometimes, it is more beneficial for the addict to get honest with "himself, God and one other" before he gets honest with his partner. In our work with hundreds of addicts, the relief that comes with finally getting honest with someone you trust about all your secrets from all your acting out (hence the value of the 4th and 5th Steps in the Program of AA (and related programs such as CA/OA/SLAA, SAA, etc.) is what brings the relief. The truth will set you free!

But don't wait forever. Assess your situation. If you have already been caught but have many more secrets, take a couple of weeks or so to prepare the information. If you think someone is about to tell your spouse, then use interim disclosure with the knowledge that if you open Pandora's box, your partner will want to look in more and more; in such a case, the help of a therapist may be in order.

The next chapter speaks more directly to the consequences of disclosure.

References

Anonymous *Hope and Recovery*. Minneapolis: CompCare Publishers, 1987.

Brown, Emily M. *Patterns of Infidelity and Their Treatment*. New York: Brunner/Mazel, 1991.

Burton-Nelson, Mariah. *The Unburdened Heart*. San Francisco: Harper, 2000.

Glass, Shirley. *Not Just Friends*. New York: Simon & Schuster, 2003.

Glass, Shirley P. and Wright, T. L. Justifications for extramarital relationships: The association between attitudes, behaviors, and gender. *The Journal of Sex Research, 29*(3): 361–387, 1992.

Herman, Judith. *Trauma and Recovery: The Aftermath of Violence from Domestic Abuse to Political Terror*. New York: Basic Books, 1992.

Schneider, Jennifer, Corley, M. Deborah, and Irons, Richard R. Surviving disclosure of infidelity: Results of an international survey of 164 recovering sex addicts and partners. *Sexual Addiction and Compulsivity, 5*, 189–217, 1998.

Schneider, Jennifer, Richard Irons, and M. Deborah Corley. Disclosure of extramarital sexual activities by sexually exploitative professionals and other persons with addictive or compulsive sexual disorders." *Journal of Sex Education and Therapy*, 24, 277-287, 1999.

Siegel, Daniel. *Emotional Intellegence*, New York: Bantam Books,1995.

Spring, Janis Abrahms. *How Can I Forgive You? The Courage to Forgive, the Freedom Not To.* New York: HarperCollins, 2005.

Tomm, Karl, Deconstructing shame and guilt; Opening space for forgiveness and reconciliation. Texas Association of Marriage and Family Therapist Annual Conference, January 2002.

Chapter Four

Consequences of Disclosure

Everyone thought that Lyndon and Loretta were the ideal couple. Married for 18 years, they were both successful health care professionals and the parents of three high achieving children. What Loretta didn't know, however, was that Lyndon had a secret life, consisting of a series of affairs with women he'd met at the hospital. Lyndon related:

> I was tired of living a double life. The lying, the sneaking around, the false reassurances to my wife whenever she questioned me,—I hated the person I had become. Finally I went to see a counselor, who recommended I join Sex Addicts Anonymous. The counselor told me I had to tell my wife if I was going to recover and that I would be wise to see a lawyer in case the situation at work created a legal problem. The guys in SAA were very supportive and that gave me some hope. However, some of the SAA members advised me to wait a year to get some clarity before disclosing to my wife, and buttressed their recommendation by quoting something from the AA Big Book supporting that position. But I loved my wife and hated that I had betrayed her. There had been so many times it had been on my lips that when my wife looked at me one day and said, "Lyndon—I'm so worried about you. You are losing weight and you are so unhappy and tormented," I broke down and told her the truth. I had not intended to, but the feeling was bigger than me.

Loretta reported:

> I felt suicidal when he told me. What would happen to our careers? What did this mean about our marriage? Would he lose his ability to prescribe or do surgery because of his actions? What would happen to our children if the media got this information? I was beside myself. I pictured killing him and then myself. I had never thought myself capable of considering those actions. If it had not been for the children, I don't know what I would have done. I felt betrayed

by the person I trusted the most. I went into shock. I was numb. Right then and there I decided the marriage was over. I removed my wedding ring and wrote him a letter telling him I was leaving and taking the children. Then I slept in a separate room because I was afraid of what I might do since all the children were out of town.

The next day, Loretta went to see a therapist who understood addictions. The therapist advised Loretta to take some time before making any final decision about her marriage. Together they agreed to spend six months clarifying Loretta's feelings, exploring her abandonment issues, and helping Loretta understand the extent of Lyndon's commitment to the marriage and more about how the addiction impacted her and their marriage. By the end of the six months she and Lyndon were attending a couples' support group and had decided to stay together.

Cary and Cynthia had a difficult marriage but had managed to stay together for 12 years. Part of the reason they were able to get through difficult times was because both had been in recovery from alcoholism for four years. Despite his sobriety from alcohol, Cary had not been able to manage his anger and frustrations when they fought or when he lost his job. A few years ago he had turned to Internet pornography and then arranging online for "escorts", some of whom provided additional sexual services like a prostitute. He rationalized this behavior as okay, that if Cynthia wouldn't have sex with him, he deserved to get some relief elsewhere. However, over time he had progressed from occasional use of escorts to frequent use of Internet pornography, masturbation, and arranging over the Internet to meet anonymous partners, including men, in places where he could receive oral sex. He knew he had to do something about this problem when one of the places he frequented was raided by the police just as he was driving into the parking lot. Cary's fears of giving Cynthia a sexually transmitted disease, such as herpes, HIV or hepatitis C, led him to seek help for his addiction and ultimately to disclose to Cynthia. "I felt a great deal of shame, and was afraid that Cynthia would leave me. But I knew I had to tell her anyway."

Cynthia reported:

I felt as if I had been deceived, betrayed, taken as a fool, victimized. I was ashamed and thought I was a "loser" for being with him because he had done these things with men. I was so afraid and angry I was beside myself for days – screaming at him, demanding an HIV and Hep C test from my doctors and alienating those people too. Then I had to take a hard look at myself. I have to admit, I hadn't been there for him—but that isn't an excuse for his actions. But at least I hadn't not been there for him because I was involved in an affair myself and now had exposed my affair partner to possible serious STDs. I had been oblivious about what was happening to him and the possible consequences my behavior might have on him. I had never stopped smoking despite saying I had on numerous occasions when he would ask me. It would have been easy for me to blame him—I did for a while. But who was I kidding! Myself! I wasn't any more sober than he was. It was so clear that I also needed more work on my recovery too.

Cynthia and Cary both renewed their commitment to recovery and began marital therapy shortly after disclosure. Both agreed that disclosure opened the door to healing their marriage and got them back on track with recovery.

Mary and Bill had been married for 15 years and had two school-aged children. Mary was a very pretty, enthusiastic, and bright woman, with no college education. Yet it seemed that no matter what she embarked upon in her career, she was successful. Bill, on the other hand, had a college degree and had been in the same job, working his way up the corporate ladder at a painfully slow pace, with only one promotion during their 15 years of marriage. To others this marriage seemed perfect. However, Mary had not been content with Bill from almost the day they were married. She was disappointed that Bill was not able to progress more quickly in his job and she longed for excitement. She wanted action; she wanted to get out and do things. Bill was just boring.

Mary had begun having sexual affairs in high school, when her biology teacher had approached her during her junior year. The attention, perceived status, and risk made this liaison exciting and set a pattern for her for years to come—older men or men in positions of power and risk taking—a formula for a greater high. For all the years of their marriage Mary had had numerous affairs, all in risky situations with older or powerful men. Over time as her career grew, she had made efforts to curb her behavior because she realized the risk taking was becoming greater and greater. But her efforts were not enough.

It all came to an end when Mary and a board member of the not-for-profit agency for whom she worked were caught in the parking lot of a cheap motel engaging in oral sex on the hood of her car. Both were arrested for indecent exposure, and the call from the police station to Bill changed both his and Mary's lives. Not only was the arrest shaming and expensive, the news media made this story front page news for several days. Their children, neighbors, and relatives all were witnesses of the handcuffed professionals being shoved into the police car. Bill chose to escape with the children to his parents' home in another state, leaving Mary behind. As further revelations about Mary's past appeared in the local press, Bill decided to relocate permanently, and the couple eventually divorced.

Even though the media coverage, an overnight stay in jail, and loss of her husband and children had been horrible for Mary, this experience became the catalyst that gave Mary the push she needed to get help and into serious recovery.

> It was clear that I was on a pathway to destruction. Actually, I destroyed lots on the way to that mess that blew up in all our faces. If this had not happened, I would have picked the wrong guy in some bar and found myself beaten, raped, or even dead in some hotel room or back alley. This has been a hard road. I lost everything that I thought was important—Bill and for a while could not even see my children. I lost my career and my so-called friends. But with the help of treatment, new friends in the program, and a renewed relationship with my Higher Power, I found myself. It is still one day at a time, but I am sober. I have another job, some real friends, a chance to be a better mom even though my kids still have problems over my behavior. Still, I finally like myself. If this had not happened, I wouldn't be here today. I am sad for those who were hurt by my actions. But I am so grateful for my recovery.

Cynthia and Cary, and Loretta and Lyndon are two couples whose relationships survived and got better through disclosure. Other couples, such as Bill and Mary, did not reunite, but despite their divorce Mary was glad the disclosure forced her to get help and into recovery.

No matter what the reason for the disclosure, it is a process rather than a one-time event. The first step is to identify and face the fears that come with disclosure.

Preparing to Manage Emotions

Emotions run rampant before, during, and after a disclosure. It is common for people to report combinations of feelings, ranging from relief and hope to rage and despair. Of course an addict who is planning a formal disclosure has been planning and rehearsing what he will say in his head or with his sponsor, a friend, or therapist. Prior to the disclosure he feels nervousness, fear, anxiety. Most addicts hope that telling will in some way help, but fear a whole host of losses and do not want to suffer the consequences.

Joe, a 43-year-old electrician and father of two children, recalled:

> *I had so much shame; I did not know how I was going to get through it. My self-worth had hit bottom and I felt like a worthless piece of shit. I was so depressed; often suicidal, but did not even have the guts to do that. I was scared she would never believe me again or worse yet, she would leave and take the kids. I couldn't blame her if she did. I felt like such a failure, like scum, horrified that I hurt her so much.*

No matter what the circumstances, you will have a variety of emotions throughout the disclosure process and in the aftermath when your partner is trying to get a handle on what to do next. It is not your job to try to change her or manage her emotional state – you are responsible for how you behave, no matter what she does. Being able to identify your emotions and then managing them in a healthy way is your task. Of course you may be angry or sad, fearful or full of shame, but knowing how you feel and then managing those feelings can make all the difference in how you are able to get through disclosure anytime during your relationship.

One way to learn about emotional states is to keep a daily journal of your thoughts. Finding the time to record and analyze all your feelings may be difficult, so we recommend once a day to actually keep track of your thoughts and feelings associated with an emotional event that happened that day.

In a nutshell, a thoughts and feelings journal documents your thoughts and feelings related to an event that happens during the day that you experience a strong emotion as a result of the event. In writing about the event, you think about what happened; who was there, what was the setting? For example, pretend your partner found a receipt from a restaurant where you had lunch with your new secretary. Because your secretary is a beautiful young woman, you omitted telling your partner about having lunch with her when your partner asked about your day; in fact, you told your partner that you had lunch with a recovery friend at a fast food place. Now your partner has the receipt and has started to confront your lying to her about where you had been at lunch. What thoughts would you have had that it would be okay not to tell her about the lunch? What would be going through your head as you saw her going through your jacket pockets, when she found the receipt, when she started having strong emotions about being lied to, and finally when she said she had had enough of your lying and stormed out the door? Circle the thoughts that may be related to your core beliefs about your partner and about yourself. Then identify the range of feelings you think you would have had in response to something like this. Which ones would be strongest, where would you feel those emotions in your body (the body is first to give you a hint that you are having a strong feeling – most people when angry tense some muscles, sometimes their stomach gets upset.) Next identify what you might have done well in this situation to manage your emotions as well as how you made things worse. Finally, make a plan about how you might do things differently if you had a chance. (This activity is sometimes called a Thoughts/Feelings Journal.)

In the above situation a **Thoughts/Feeling Journal** might go something like this:

Event: Jill found receipt in my pocket, came storming into the den and confronted me, yelling that I lied to her.

Thoughts: I can't believe her – she is snooping and jumping to conclusions just like she *always* does. Why do I have to tell her everything? That lunch was just with my secretary but Jill will never believe me no matter what I say or what evidence I give her. I sure don't want to have to tell my secretary all about this just to keep Jill satisfied. Damn her – when is she going to get over this?

Feelings: Fear, anger, shame, regret

Body sensations: Tighten jaw and grit teeth as she yells; heart begins to race; face gets flushed; stomach cramps.

This is what I did well: Did not go further than just having lunch with secretary. I caught myself getting defensive. I took two deep breaths to try to slow my heart rate while Jill was losing it. Let her yell, tried not to get into blaming her more – after all, I did lie by omission. I agreed that she has a right to be mad; reminded myself I had not had a relapse, but was on a slippery slope. I asked for a time-out until we both were calmer. We agreed on time to meet.

Here are the ways I made things worse: Went to lunch alone with secretary in first place, and then lied about it. Got defensive immediately and started blaming Jill for going through my things. Stopped listening for a couple of minutes and started justifying my actions in my head, looking at what Jill had done wrong instead of where I need to be accountable, started planning my retaliation plan. Started thinking of how I could manipulate her through shaming her about her lack of support.

Plan of action: Think through any action in the first place that would look like or actually be the first steps toward doing behaviors connected to my addiction. – Examine the thoughts section of the journal. Identify my thinking errors. Actively search for information or evidence that contradicts the thoughts or supports the thoughts.

For example - The receipt was suspicious and she has every right not to trust me given my long history of lying. I don't have to tell her everything, but it is helpful to keep her informed of things I'm doing that might appear suspicious. I also don't have to tell my secretary, but I might be wise to give her some information so it would be easier to call Jill during those lunches to verify who I am with and why.

Plan of Action: This is what you plan to do to help this situation and plan for next time.

Example: Apologize for not telling her before about the lunch and for yelling at her. Discuss this with my therapist and sponsor to make certain I am not "fooling" myself. Plan not to have lunch alone with any women, even my secretary, unless it is necessary and on those cases to call Jill and better yet, tell her in advance.

This may seem like a lot, but practicing this skill will help. Learning to manage your emotional states will help no matter where you are in the process of disclosure or recovery. It is a great tool to have and if you practice using the thoughts-feeling journal every day, you will find you are better able to quickly find and correct thinking errors so you don't waste time obsessing over things you can do nothing about. It also helps you see when you need to give your partner information so trust can be rebuilt.

One other thing – you will notice in the section on what you did right, there is mention of taking deep breaths until your heart rate slowed. This is an excellent tip for managing emotions. When people get angry or scared (usually both are happening, with anger just masking the fear), their heart rate goes up. If your heart rate exceeds 100, your ability to access the area of your brain that helps you think rationally is gone! Take that big breath, focus on the exhale and slow it down – that will slow your heart and relax your muscles. Decreasing your heart rate allows your brain to access its common sense and problem solving areas, so if you can't manage your emotions, ask for a time out to calm yourself. Otherwise, you will be caught in the emotional fight or flight part of the brain that shifts to automatic pilot and old and ineffective ways of responding to fear and anger.

Positive Outcomes of Disclosure

If disclosure had only the negative consequences reported later in this chapter, it is unlikely that addicts, partners, and couples who have been through this experience would recommend it to others. In our survey we asked addicts and partners if they thought disclosure was the right thing to do. We asked them to think both retrospectively about how they felt at the time of the disclosure and how they felt about it when they completed the survey, which was weeks to years afterwards. Thinking back to the time of the disclosure, over 80 percent of the partners and more than 60 percent of the addicts reported they felt at the time that it was the right thing to do. The next statistic is even more impressive. At the time of the survey, that number had risen significantly. *Of the partners, 93 percent felt it had been the right thing to do. And a whopping 96 percent of the addicts felt disclosure was the right thing to do!* Despite all the pain and loss, enough good had to come out of the process for people to feel so strongly that it was the right thing to do and the majority said they would recommend disclosure to other couples.

In our study, addicts reported the following as positive aspects of disclosure:

- Honesty frees you

- End to denial

- Hope for the future of the relationship

- A chance for the partner to get to know the addict better

- A new start for the addict, whether in the same relationship or not

Sydney, writing two years after his original disclosure, said,

In some ways the disclosure was selfish. I couldn't stand the pain of the double life. This is who I really am. I had been so manipulative she had no idea the depth of my emptiness or my compulsive use of prescription drugs for so many years, working at a job that used me, trying to be the somebody I wasn't, trying to fill that void. Disclosure was proof that I had a real chance to stop my out-of-control behavior because I could not continue on the course my life was taking if I wanted to live.

Jeffrey, who had been through a painful disclosure, reflected,

The disclosure hurt, was more traumatic than I thought possible, yet at the same time the information was sort of a relief because now I knew I wasn't going crazy. My instincts were accurate, he had lied for years. For about two years I had suspected something. I can now understand the past, it helped me understand why he acted the way he did. I felt relieved to finally know the truth. Now I could make choices based on the truth, not some lies.

Echoing a common theme reported by partners, Lydia, aged 38 recalled,

The disclosure let me know he cared about me enough to share that difficult information. It meant he loved me enough to be honest

with me. I saw it as an opportunity to seek help. This might be a beginning.

According to Eldon,

I was so tired. Porn on the Internet owned me. I found myself in such physical and emotional pain realizing I had snuck out of bed so many nights to spend most of the night looking for that never obtainable high again, masturbating until I was numb, back hurting, dehydrated and realizing that I had to try to sleep a half hour and get up for work. I did not have to keep on living with this secret, feeling so shitty all the time – I had to get some help. Though I had admitted to some use before, through the full disclosure and my honesty about how I was really feeling, I found out my partner really loved me and was willing to go to therapy with me and help me solve my problems with this addiction.

Peter recognized,

It meant that I had to admit to myself and my wife that I was gay. My marriage of 27 years ended, but it was not really an adverse consequence. It was the right thing for both of us. We survived it and remained friends.

Adverse Consequences of the Disclosure

Although the above responses reflect the feelings of hope, the relief for partners to finally gain clarity about the past, and the recognition by some addicts that living a double life was more destructive than was opening up, we will not gloss over the intense feelings people have during this process. Just like the majority of addicts, partners also recommended disclosure. Yet, partners also reported that each went through what seemed like the worst nightmare of their lives. Recent studies have reported symptoms that reflect the trauma most partners suffer when disclosure, especially disclosure when they had been told in the past that nothing was wrong or received only a partial disclosure.

Mary, 42, had a traumatic reaction:

I felt like I'd been stabbed right through the heart; the pain took my breath away. I didn't feel that I could breathe or would live. I felt frozen in time; I had overwhelming terror about what would happen next. I was paranoid about everything and had no faith in my ability to make decisions. I couldn't sleep, couldn't concentrate, wasn't able to take care of my kids or anything else – I just fell apart for a while.

For many partners, the impact of the addiction which comes to light through the disclosure represents an attachment injury, wherein the relationship becomes a source of danger instead of a safe haven in times of emotional distress. When an attachment bond is violated or broken, the person often suffers pain that we call *relational trauma*. As in any other trauma, initially the partner may respond in one of two ways – she will either make a valiant attempt to get the spouse to reconnect or will build an emotional wall shutting out the addict, never allowing herself to be vulnerable again.

As we stated earlier, both addicts and partners reported intense emotional pain as part of the disclosure process. As with all pain, it is a chance to grow and learn but it is not without risk.

Revealing secrets is especially a traumatic experience for your partner. Knowing you have been lied to is bound to cause pain; knowing you have lied repeatedly to the person you love causes guilt and shame. When the secret activities have been sexual, the pain and the sense of betrayal are more acute. Partners often seriously consider the likelihood that the relationship will not survive the truth about the addict's behavior. Adding insult to injury, there are cases in which an arrest has been made, financial security lost, or a life-threatening or incurable disease may have been transmitted. Sometimes addicts have another totally separate life, with another family, children who see the addict as a father and for whom the addict has financial responsibility. If there are legal consequences with law enforcement or the Internal Revenue Service, or if the addict has lost his or her job, both you and your partner are plunged further into fear.

The anger or resentment the partner feels because of this threat is sometimes insurmountable. In addition, the core fear of abandonment that many partners of addicts feel is often triggered by the disclosure. You can expect that disclosure will be a traumatic experience, that the family will change, and that the consequences of your behaviors may last for years. We will now review what these adverse consequences are for each of you:

Adverse Consequences for the Addict

Addicts who reveal their secret life to their partners can expect to experience some of the following adverse consequences:

- Worsening of the couple relationship

- Guilt and shame

- Anger and sometimes rage from the partner

- Loss of trust by the partner

- Limiting access to the children

- Cutting off of the sexual relationship

- Damage to other relationships, such as with children or friends

- Legal consequences

- Loss of job

Steven, 36, who had been in recovery from nicotine, alcohol, benzodiazepines, and sex addiction for five years, relapsed when a friend showed him how to get around the filter on his computer and view the extremes that existed in pornography websites. Just when he thought it couldn't get better, his friend showed him how to engage in interactive sexual sites using his webcam. Steven was immediately drawn to the excitement of actually seeing someone do what he commanded. Before long he found himself smoking again at the computer. After several offline hookups, during which he resumed drinking, he returned to AA where his old sponsor told him he needed to tell his wife. But the disclosure brought consequences Steven had not expected:

> There were fights before but now she had the ammunition she needed to keep me in line. She didn't trust me anymore. The doubt about what I might have done or might do in the future was debilitating—she tried to control my behavior to prevent my acting out. She was continually accusing me of affairs, acting out – even accused me of using crystal meth even though I hadn't gone that far. It was a nightmare for her and for me.

After admitting her affairs to her husband, 37-year old Suzy told us,

My husband wanted to 'reclaim' me sexually. I felt so guilty that I let him consume me sexually for weeks. Then I became disgusted and started shutting him out. He then became vigilant about my behavior, thoughts, and actions for several months. He started to judge me and try to manage my program. Now when he is feeling insecure or mad, he brings up my history and throws up certain situations or individuals to me. I don't know what to say; I just feel worse, guiltier.

Other addicts complained that their partner was monitoring their every movement, or constantly reminding them of past transgressions, or withholding sex as punishment or because the partner did not feel safe. These behaviors by the partner are normal and to be expected after the trauma of betrayal.

Initially after disclosure, adverse consequences for both addicts and partners that usually disappear after a period of time include sleep loss and obsessive thinking, loss of appetite, stomach pain, diarrhea, sometimes vomiting, and weight loss. Worry and lack of concentration interfere with work performance and day-to-day tasks. It is as though someone close to you died and the grief crashes over you like a tidal wave. Not being able to focus makes everything harder. Depression makes decision-making difficult; making mistakes is common. Car accidents are common.

It is not unusual for an addict to lose his or her job as a result of acting out at work or as a result of public exposure of some illegal acting out. Sometimes illegal behaviors lead to formal charges against the addict, huge legal costs, and even incarceration.

The financial consequences can also be immense. Therapy and treatment are expensive; legal costs even more so. If job loss is a consequence, then financial problems are even greater. Often acting out has been associated with spending money—on pornography, prostitutes, gifts, drugs, and alcohol. Some addicts have led such a double life that they have another household set up; some even have other children to support. But the truth of the matter is, *even without disclosure most addicts experience these consequences.* You need to realize that the worst consequences are a result of the addiction experience, not the admission.

Adverse Consequences of Disclosure for the Partner

For the partner, the feelings are so intense she (or he) thinks her head or heart will explode. She may feel a combination of anger, grief, confusion, pain, fear, and sometimes revulsion. The obsession that invaded her brain takes a new turn. Before, she might have suspected something, but now the obsession turns to worrying about how she missed it, what is wrong with her that this happened, and concern about what will happen in the future.

Theresa, a 43-year-old cashier and mother of three, reported,

> *I couldn't believe what I was hearing. This was the man that I thought I could trust. This was my life, blowing up in front of me. I had never doubted myself any more than I did at that moment. What was wrong with me that something like this could happen? And how did I miss something this big? Then afterward, I lost my relationship with my family when they found out. I would have flashbacks of him telling and I couldn't stop the hurt, the loneliness, the isolation I felt. I couldn't tell anyone for the longest time. I couldn't sleep. I felt so old and tired, worn out. Not only couldn't I trust him with drugs and alcohol and money, now if he used it meant he would be using crack in some hotel, wearing my clothes, and masturbating to some porn on the cable TV. God . . . How the hell do you get beyond that?*

Among the adverse consequences the partner can expect as a result of disclosure are:

- A worsening of the couple relationship

- Depression and even suicidal thoughts

- Attempts to compensate for the pain with acting-out behaviors such as drug use and sex

- Loss of self-esteem

- Decreased ability to concentrate or to function at work

- Feelings of shame and guilt

- Distrust of everyone

- Anger and rage

- Fear of abandonment

- Physical illness

- Lack of sexual desire

Some partners reported becoming depressed, distracted, and even suicidal. According to Phil, whose partner had starting having sex with other men when using crystal methamphetamine, supposedly for weight loss:

> I couldn't concentrate. I got into two car accidents and did things like putting milk in the cupboard and cereal in the refrigerator. I was afraid I would drive off a particular bridge and was afraid I would hurt myself with a kitchen knife.

Millie's husband told her a project at work required him to stay late for several months. In reality, he was spending hours every evening in cybersex activities in his office. He exchanged and downloaded S & M pornographic pictures on his work computer, engaged in real-time online sex involving bondage and domination, and occasionally had real-life sexual assignations with women he'd "met" online. After learning of her husband's double life, Millie said,

> I felt total distrust in myself, in him, in the relationship. I felt betrayed, confused, afraid, stunned that the person I loved and trusted most in the world had lied about who he was, and that I had lived through some vast and sinister cover-up.

Other partners described their insecurity and loss of self-esteem at feeling unable to compete with sexual partners, the power of drugs, or the seduction of gambling or high-risk spending. Some partners have to have time away to think and let the anger subside. Sometimes there is a feeling of being suffocated by the presence of the addict.

Marie, whose husband had spent hundreds of hours on the Internet experimenting with various illegal sexual practices, including viewing teen pornography and engaging in sex with minors, explained,

> I was so devastated and repulsed by him. I didn't want him to touch me; I hated him and wanted him to leave. I loathed him and wanted him dead. The betrayal on all levels was just more than I could take.

Samantha's spouse of 20 years revealed a long history of unprotected sex with prostitutes while using cocaine. For years they had struggled to make ends meet. Time and time again she had had to explain to her children that there was no money for new school clothes or toys at Christmas. This information brought back all the sadness from those times of deprivation.

> I'd been victimized and I took it personally. He could have killed me with HIV. It was like someone had taken a shotgun and blasted me all over, the pain was unbearable and I couldn't stand to be around him. I was embarrassed and humiliated. I couldn't bear to think what to tell the kids—how do I explain to them that they mean so little to their father that he would spend money we did not have just to please himself. I hate him and myself for being with him.

Some couples experience several separations and reconciliations: "Sometimes I thought I was going crazy. He would move out for three or four months and then back in to figure out what HE wanted. I suffered abandonment each time and waited for him to make up his mind. Neither of us had enough recovery to deal with it."

Some partners use alcohol and other drugs to "soften the blow." This can be a time of high risk for relapse by partners who are also addicts. Some partners have more sex with the addict because of their fear of losing him or to prove they can keep up. Others get involved in a revenge affair, sometimes disclosing and other times keeping their own secret. Too often partners report that they end up in a liaison with someone they have turned to for help such as a work colleague, a friend of the addict, and in some cases even the attorney, physician, or therapist from whom they are seeking professional services. A rebound affair was reported by several partners. After the first rush of intensity, this did not prove to be a constructive solution to the couple's problems: It complicated their efforts to put the relationship back together, caused additional distrust, and often resulted in depression for one or both partners.

Friends frequently choose sides and, depending on how much is disclosed to them, can share information that should be private with people who do not need to know. Family members often side with the partner and are incensed when she doesn't leave, so they sever the relationship. This is yet another disruption and often very painful for the partner and the children. If acting out behaviors are illegal, sometimes children are removed from the home—an extremely traumatizing event for children which compounds the pain of the betrayal.

Do Partners Leave As A Result of Disclosure?

Most addicted persons worry that they will lose the relationship, and the fear that the partner will leave is a huge deterrent to disclosure by the addict. But do partners actually leave? Threats to leave are a common, easily understood reaction by partners who are shocked to learn that their mate has betrayed them with another person. About 70 percent of partners have some suspicions about the addict's behavior long before the addict admits the secrets. Some partners confront their mate; others keep quiet either because the addict has said it was their imagination, or they fear the consequences of saying anything. They may want to avoid confrontation at all costs, or else because they feel everything is their fault. Norma reported,

> I had a few suspicions, just a feeling. I tried to ignore it and look at the good in our relationship. Finally I brought my feelings to him and said I felt suspicious. I proceeded to tell him that it must be just me, that I might need to get help. He let me take all the guilt and blame on myself, though he was the one using.

Those who do confront are sometimes met with active resistance. Sylvia, now divorced, wrote,

> I was very naive and out of touch. A part of me knew that he was doing weird stuff and he even told me in subtle ways about it, but I wanted to minimize it all. When I told him about my fears, he would get extremely violent and throw things and break things and refuse to talk to me.

Jeremy related,

> When I told Betty about my suspicions, she threw a fit. She accused me of not trusting her, said that if I wasn't satisfied I was free to move out, and stormed out of the house, leaving me with the four kids. She didn't return until next morning. I didn't say a word about it after that.

Lorelei, the wife of a physician mentioned in Chapter 3 who had multiple affairs, said,

> *I had suspicions because he would not answer his cell phone and would come home late, sometimes reeking of cigarette smoke and alcohol. He would blatantly deny doing anything wrong. He'd be insulted that I questioned him and would often manipulate the scene and argue that I was pathetic and paranoid. Sometimes I would back down and actually apologize for accusing him. Then I would feel a terrible guilt.*

Confrontation and denial are a recurrent theme in the relationships of addicts and their partners. These result in a pattern of dishonesty by the addict and distrust by the partner, which subsequently makes it difficult for the couple to restore trust in their relationship.

In many cases, suspicions about secret activities result in threats to leave even before any disclosure is made. About 40 percent of partners make such threats, which understandably gives pause to men and women who are considering disclosing their secrets.

Receiving a disclosure can be painful, terrifying, hurtful, anger-provoking, and possibly the worst thing a person has ever experienced. Our research indicated what we have seen clinically for years: For some, the information is just too much to take. The partner feels wounded and has no interest in trying further, leaves or demands the addict leave and takes steps to obtain a divorce.

Although some partners immediately close ranks with the addict and promise support, a majority (60 percent in our study) threaten to leave or to end the marriage or committed relationship. However, a large majority of partners (72 percent in our study) do not act on this threat. Among those who do separate, about half eventually reunite. For those who seek separation first, this seems to allow enough distance for both the addict and partner to seek support and help. Addicts new to recovery require intense focus on their recovery programs; partners have equally difficult times healing from the trauma of the addict's behavior and need time and space to practice self care. While not all separations are temporary, even couples who end their relationship often remain friendly and co-parent in healthier ways. So separation initially isn't all bad.

Partners are just as likely as addicts to come from dysfunctional families in which their own childhood needs for nurturing were not met. They may believe that love must be earned by giving. They may have been initially attracted to the addict because this was a person who seemed to carry childhood wounds, who needed to be helped, or whose family background was familiar.

Many partners of addicts have childhood wounds that result in a great fear of abandonment. Life without the addict may seem like a fate worse than death. Although they may threaten to leave as a result of receiving a painful disclosure, some partners are unable to take effective action because of their own fears. They may conclude that living with the pain is better than living alone, or may decide to give the addict "another chance." Some rationalize their lack of action; others simply postpone making a real decision. Still others have to consider the consequences of leaving on their children and financial situation, so stay almost out of default. This rarely turns out to be a good thing for anyone if the partner is not also able to get support and help.

Threats Before and After Disclosure

Partners who threaten to leave when they only suspect infidelity might be expected to threaten to leave once their suspicions are confirmed. Interestingly, however, about a quarter of partners who threaten to leave on the basis of suspicions *before* disclosure do not make the same threat following disclosure. The reasons given by two women were:

> I was so happy he was finally in recovery that I felt we could make it as a couple.

> I stayed because of the serious level of his addictions—I believe he is so sick. I could not think of breaking up our relationship as long as he is 100 percent committed to a serious recovery program.

Although some partners threaten to leave, often they will demand the addict get therapy and attend 12-step meetings. Many times during the process, the therapist will invite the partner to a few sessions or will refer the addict and partner to another therapist for couple's therapy. This can represent an opportunity for the couple to learn new ways of relating and help them get back on track to a happier life.

Conclusions

Disclosure of secrets, especially painful secrets involving sexual activity with others, usually precipitates a crisis in the couple's relationship and an initial worsening of the relationship. Both partners and addicts experience a series of adverse consequences. In addition to possible legal, health, and job consequences, the addict typically feels guilt and shame, anger at the partner, resentment that the partner no longer trusts and may now keep him (or her) on a short leash. The addict often has to go through a period where the partner is not interested in a sexual relationship.

Partners who have been on the receiving end of a disclosure typically experience depression and even suicidal thoughts, fear of abandonment, loss of self-esteem, decreased ability to concentrate or to function at work, distrust of the addict and perhaps of everyone, anger, lack of sexual desire, physical illness, and at times, attempts to compensate for the pain with acting-out behaviors such as misuse of food, drug use, and sex. As part of their distress and anger, many partners react to the disclosure by threatening to leave. Fear of this possibility can prevent addicts from revealing secrets, even if they wish to unburden themselves as part of their own recovery process.

The good news, as we learned from many couples that have been through this process, is that most people who threaten to leave don't do so. Even when the couple does separate, the chances are good that they will reunite if each is committed to their individual recovery from their addiction and trauma. Disclosure can lay the groundwork for a new relationship, based on honesty and greater intimacy.

In later chapters we will describe how counselors can facilitate disclosure, what couples who have been through the process recommend to other couples, how much to reveal and when, and what tools of recovery are helpful for rebuilding trust and restoring the relationship. To prepare, we'd like to ask you to think about the following questions as they apply to your own life:

- What do you fear the most about telling?

- What sources of strength do you have to get you through this time?

- Who can you call to support you during this time?

- What skills do you need to improve to handle the disclosure?

The next chapter gives steps for a formal disclosure.

References

Corley, M. D. & Schneider, J. P. Partner reactions to disclosure of relapse by self-identified sexual addicts. *Sexual Addiction and Compulsivity*, 2012, in press.

Glass, Shirley. *NOT Just Friends.* The Free Press, New York, NY, 2003

Schneider, J.P., Corley, M.D., and Irons, R.R. Surviving disclosure of infidelity: Results of an international survey of 164 recovering sex addicts and their partners. *Sexual Addiction and Compulsivity* 5:189–217, 1998.

Chapter Five

The Formal Disclosure: How to Do It Right

Most initial disclosures are not planned. They are prompted either by external events such as a partner's suspicions or discovery, or by being confronted by an employer, neighbor, or the police because of some illegal behavior; or else by intense internal emotions that can no longer be tolerated. Depending on the specific circumstances, the addict's personality, his current emotional state, and his fears of the outcome, he may disgorge the entire story, replete with details; alternatively, he may attempt damage control by revealing as little as possible.

In Jordan's case, he had denied his wife's suspicions of this affair and others and had given great thought about how to keep the situation secret as long as possible. When the time came, disclosure did not come off as he thought. As he put it, "The first disclosure was not pretty, but at least I told Jada. The second disclosure was not too pretty either, but the truth that came out of it was beautiful for me. Without that truth, we could not have survived what happened."

Jordan never thought his life would come to this. He had fulfilled his childhood dream of being a pilot and now worked for a major airline. Everything he had planned had fallen into place. He had a wonderful career doing exactly what he loved to do; he had a terrific teenaged daughter and he was married to a beautiful woman. Yet, after hitting forty, he had noticed that life just wasn't as fun or fulfilling anymore—no matter what he tried. This changed at his twenty-year class reunion.

It was at the reunion that he reconnected with Deondra , an old girlfriend who was more than a little interested in him. Her interest made him suddenly feel young again. She was a gorgeous, successful business woman who was not shy about inviting him to be sexual with her to see "if it was as good as it used to be!"

Being a pilot, Jordan could arrange to fly anywhere and, conveniently, his schedule allowed for a particularly long layover where Deondra lived. He had had numerous casual affairs for many years without Jada's knowledge, so he had no problem calling Deondra at the first opportunity. She was thrilled and anxious to see him. Soon they were seeing each other two or three times per month and calling each other daily. They were careful to leave no trail and only called on disposable cell phones, thinking nothing could be traced. Deondra soon believed it was "true love" and often told Jordan that they were "soul mates" and had a "perfect" relationship. They were always glad to see each other, never fought, and to Jordan, the sex seemed just like his fantasies in the pornography he regularly viewed on his laptop when away from home. Even though they both drank excessively during the times they were together, Deondra seemed sexually insatiable, always playful, enthusiastic, and willing to try anything.

This affair went on for almost three years. Jordan spent thousands of dollars on plane tickets for Deondra to meet him in various places, on the disposable cell phones, and on many gifts. Not new to the need to be very careful when having affairs, he was always careful to buy his wife the same gift so if Jada ever found a receipt, he could claim it was the gift for her and the store must have made a mistake and charged him twice. When Jada questioned him about the money he had taken from his savings account, he concocted various excuses such as buying parts for the classic Chevy he was refurbishing in the garage.

Soon Deondra and Jordan began to fantasize about him leaving Jada for a life together. Jordan did love Deondra but did not know how he could leave his wife and the fifteen years of history they had together, yet he did not know what to say to her or to Deondra about his ambivalence. In an attempt to make Deondra more secure so she'd back off some on her demands for a long term commitment, he began to talk as if he would leave Jada sometime in the future. Meanwhile, he took no action except to drink more to relieve his anxiety. The more time he spent with Deondra, the more time she wanted. Meanwhile, back at home his wife and daughter were complaining about how distracted he had become and about the time he spent locked in his garage (phoning Deondra) when he was home. Jordan was not sure what to do. There was just not enough of him to go around.

Jordan's life really fell apart when he agreed to meet Deondra for a "quickie" at an airport in a city she was visiting for business. She was so sexually excited when she saw him that she insisted they go to the rental car in the parking garage. Having little time and loving the thrill of the risk involved in being in a car in such a public place, Jordan felt wildly excited just hearing her talk about her desire to give him oral sex. About the time she began, he closed his eyes as he leaned back to enjoy this interlude between flights; they were so involved that neither Jordan nor Deondra noticed the police officer who had approached the car. When the officer knocked on the window and asked, "Is everything okay in there?" Deondra quickly raised her head and completely exposed Jordan. The officer demanded they immediately get out of the car, hands up. He informed Jordan and Deondra they were both in serious trouble, that it was against the law to expose oneself in a public place. Jordan could see his career and family pass before his face. He begged the officer not to arrest him, immediately inventing the story that he was an Air Force reservist about to leave the country on assignment and enjoying a last few minutes with his girlfriend. The officer escorted Jordan and Deondra into the terminal, charged him with public indecency, and then left them with airport security. Jordan missed his flight, so it was not long before his whole crew knew what had happened. Jordan was suspended until an investigation could be completed.

Deondra was beside herself with fear and shame. Jordan told her he would call as soon as he could. Fearful of losing his job, his wife, and his daughter, Jordan decided he had to end the affair with Deondra. Upon arriving home, he called Deondra and told her he loved her but that he had to end the affair. Deondra was hysterical and reminded him of their plans to be together. She suggested that this might be just the opportunity to end his marriage. Jordan told Deondra that it had been a wake-up call and that he realized he loved his wife and couldn't see her anymore. Deondra couldn't accept this, and kept calling, even to his home.

Unsure of what to do, Jordan feigned illness for the next several days in order to justify his absence from work. He did not want to hurt

Jada but wasn't sure what to say. A week after the incident, he received a certified letter from Deondra containing documentation that she was pregnant and threatening to sue him unless he left Jada and married her. Jordan knew that his life was out of control and he had to tell Jada about his secret life.

That night over dinner in a restaurant, surrounded by many people and after drinking four martinis to bolster his courage, Jordan began by announcing to Jada he had something really bad to tell her. Alarmed, fearing he had some serious health condition, she put her wine down and stared at him with tears in her eyes. Jordan said,

> *Jada, I have been really horrible. I had an affair with Deondra from the class reunion but it's over now. But the situation is really a mess. I haven't been sick, just avoiding telling you that I got suspended last week because we were caught with her giving me oral sex in a car at the airport—all of the crew knows. She wanted me to leave you and marry her. Really she trapped me with sex and now she is claiming she is pregnant and that I am the father. I have talked to our attorney and he is advising me to go to a treatment center for a month, thinking that I drank so much during this affair that I might have a drinking problem that impaired my thinking. Anyway, I have to leave tomorrow morning. I knew I had to tell you before I left. I love you, not her and I am sorry for messing up our lives.*

Jada was so shocked by Jordan's words that she threw her wine on him and stormed out of the restaurant, after telling him he need not come home. She refused to talk to him during the first three weeks he was in treatment. It was their attorney who helped her see that avoiding him and the situation wouldn't change things. She agreed to talk to him and to attend the family therapy at the treatment center.

In treatment, Jordan followed the steps outlined in this chapter to present a formal disclosure to Jada. She was able to process the disclosure with therapists and with him. It was here that Jada realized much had been going on in her life and marriage that she had not paid attention to. When she returned from the family session, she joined a support group and began her own therapy. It was extremely difficult for her for the first several months of her therapy. Upon Jordan's return, they both attended individual and couple's therapy. Realizing that other couples also faced similar tragic circumstances, they found the strength and support to sustain them during the challenging months to resolve the problems resulting from Jordan's actions.

Jordan and Jada have now been married almost 25 years. Their daughter has completed school and is training to be a pilot herself. They provide financial support for the baby born to Jordan and Deondra and enjoy having him as part of their family during various holidays and each summer. They were lucky, but there were many consequences. Jordan lost his job with the airline. He was able to find a job as a private pilot of a person in recovery, but not before Jada's parents found out and encouraged her to leave him. Their daughter struggled with school and emotional distress for several months. Jada was plagued with flashbacks and weeks of insomnia. Luckily, they had the resources for all who were involved to get therapy. Both agreed that the second disclosure and the therapy everyone got helped them start from an honest place in their marriage. With that beginning, lots of faith in a Higher Power, and support from the friends they finally disclosed to, it was possible to start a new way of living. See Jordan's second disclosure in the box below:

Jordan's Second Disclosure

(This letter was read during a family session while Jordan was in treatment.)

Dear Jada,

I know I have disclosed some of the "facts" to you but I did not do a very good job. I am sorry about the way I told you those things. Once again, I was selfish and did not consider the impact on you. Now, I want you to know the truth about everything and am willing to answer any questions you have now or in the future.

First, I tell you these things with a heavy heart. I know you always thought we had a good marriage. What happened and is happening is not fair to you or our daughter. What I did was wrong and I am sorry you are suffering the consequences for what I did. It isn't fair and I can't expect you to forgive me.

I want you to know, you did not do anything to cause what has happened. I made the choices I made because of the way I was thinking. That is not your fault; it is mine. You are a good woman, a good wife, and a good mother. I do not blame you or anyone else for what has happened. I am responsible. Deondra did not trick me, I did what I did because I was selfish and thought the rules did not apply to me. I was wrong.

I have learned lots about myself since I came to treatment. One of the things is that I am a liar. I have lied to boost myself up. I did not want to admit and sure did not want anyone, especially you, to know how insecure I felt. I have been a liar for so long; I don't know when I started and haven't always known when I was telling a lie. It is important that you know I do know now and am remembering how much I lied to you. I lied about how I was feeling, I lied about money, where I was, the people I was with. I told lies that suggested that you were at fault, or stupid for suspecting me. Remember when you asked me about the perfume you smelled on my uniform so often and I said you were paranoid, that it was just perfume from sitting next to a flight attendant on the bus. I was wrong to have lied and I am sorry for all the times I made you question yourself. It must have made you feel crazy at times. You were not crazy or stupid or foolish then and you are not now.

You were right to suspect me. I have had several affairs since we have been married. As well as I can remember, the affairs started after I got that "ass-chewing" from one of the dads at Shari's soccer game. I felt like everyone on that field thought I was a fool and just couldn't get it out of my mind. Instead of going to you to talk about it, I picked up a flight attendant who had been telling me all about her marital problems for weeks. Most of the women have been flight attendants. I have not been with anyone that you are friends with or that you know other than Deondra and I think you only met her briefly at the class reunion. That is where I hooked up with her and started seeing her shortly thereafter.

I have spent thousands of dollars that should have gone for things for you and Shari. I have put my career in jeopardy and by doing so have put your future and Shari's future in jeopardy. I was horrible to do so and I am sorry. Our attorney tells me my supervisor is seeing my time in treatment as favorable, but I will not know the outcome of the suspension until I am finished with treatment. I am sorry for placing you in this position. I know you must be worried about what to do next.

The most difficult thing for me to admit is that I have had unprotected sex with many of these women. Not only have I exposed you to sexually transmitted diseases, there is a baby on the way who will be my financial responsibility. I have had an HIV test and it has come back negative, but if you have not had one yet, you should.

I would not blame you if you wanted a divorce. I do not want that, but I would understand how you may feel like you can never trust me again.

I hope my honesty here and my behaviors from this point forward will help you see that I am serious about our marriage. I want to be your best friend. I know you thought we were, but I wasn't. I understand that honesty is the major quality of a best friend. That is where I have to start—not just for you and our marriage, but for my own sanity.

I can't expect you to forgive me but I am hoping that you will give me a chance to re-establish a new, healthier relationship with you. I love you and Shari with all my heart.

Love, Jordan

Not all disclosures end happily, but as we've said before, the majority of couples interviewed agreed they were glad they disclosed. This was true even if the relationship ended. Ideally, disclosure allows people to make decisions based on accurate information instead of lies.

It is important to point out that disclosures do change everything and in the beginning change creates stress. The family dynamics change. Sometimes, like in Jordan and Jada's case, another child is involved and therefore another family. Careers are involved. Finances are affected. People at work or in the neighborhood often find out and unimagined consequences can result. So be prepared for changes.

How and What to Tell

Most therapists agree that a sign of recovery for an addict is when he is able to take full responsibility for what he has done. Judith Herman, author of *Trauma and Recovery: The Aftermath of Violence - From Domestic Abuse to Political Terror*, states "true forgiveness cannot be granted until the perpetrator has sought and earned it though confession, repentance, and restitution." In *The Unburdened Heart*, Mariah Burton-Nelson agrees that forgiveness requires confession and restitution, but adds that if reconciliation of an intimate relationship is desired, then remorse is also necessary. In his book, *The Science of Trust*, John Gottman agrees that the first phase of work for healing to occur for the victim of a betrayal and for the marriage is for the perpetrator of the betrayal to express remorse, establish ways to be transparent in all the perpetrator does in order to create understanding, acceptance and start the path towards forgiveness.

Confession is acknowledging your behaviors while taking full responsibility for what you have done. It is tempting to confess by phone or via a letter sent through the mail or a text. It takes more courage to be accountable face-to-face, to directly confront the other person's expression of pain or anger or grief—but that is the more effective and desirable way to do it.

Expressing genuine remorse means taking responsibility for your actions and verifying what your partner has probably suspected all along but that you have lied about. Your partner will feel like she doesn't really know who you are and can't trust you. It takes time and your demonstrated transparency for her to realize that your behavior has changed. (If you do not change your behavior, all the work you put into the disclosure will be another betrayal to your partner.)

In creating transparency, you do not want to destroy the fragile state of rebuilding trust, so you have to have no more secrets. It is important for your partner to be honest as well, but in this crisis phase, she will be expecting you to be remorseful, contrite and pay restitution in some ways. At a later time, with the help of your therapist, you may want to inquire from your partner what would be meaningful to her in the way of restitution. It is impossible for you to take back the hurt, but demonstrating that you are willing to atone for your betrayal can be important to some partners.

Prepare by first writing a letter or outline of what you want to say. A letter or written work helps you stay on track. It is okay to write a letter that at a later date you read aloud to your partner and then give to her. Reading your work also provides a starting and stopping place so that interrupting and getting off track is not as easy.

Taking responsibility for one's actions and demonstrating remorse make a disclosure more effective than just dumping on a partner. This is the first step of restitution, a process that will be described further in Chapter 9.

In the following example, Dan is a person who was willing to admit what he had done, but had trouble taking responsibility. Dan had been married to Delia for ten years. Over the years he had alternated between excessive use of alcohol, cocaine, and nicotine and was an occasional gambler. Eventually he settled on a combination of heavy cigarette smoking while drinking and masturbating to pornography. Dan had been in therapy and even gone to treatment before for his alcohol use but did not come clean to the treatment team or to Delia about the extent of his compulsive sexual activities. After treatment he would act contrite, go to Twelve-step meeetings and talk talk to his AA sponsor, but he never did fully disclose to anyone the range of his addictive behaviors. Eventually, the desire to start acting out sexually would return along with his cocaine use. Dan and Delia separated for six months following one of his binge uses while he was gambling. His persistent efforts to woo her back and his declarations of evidence that he was attending Twelve-step meetings eventually persuaded Delia to give the marriage another try.

A year after their reconciliation, Dan fell into a pattern of using cocaine, then masturbating to Internet pornography or visiting chat rooms where the conversations were sexually explicit. He eventually began emailing and texting women he met in chat rooms on the computer. Caught in fantasy, he eventually became infatuated with a young woman who lived 2,000 miles away, and flew across the country to meet her. It wasn't long before Delia discovered his porn use and the long distance encounter. This time Delia filed for divorce. After a month of a long distance romance, Dan realized what he had lost. He begged Delia to let him return. He said he was sorry, he'd do anything to make it up to her, and he suggested that they go see a therapist for a session in which Delia could tell him all the ways he had hurt her, while he would listen without defending himself. Delia declined; she had already told him dozens of times over the years how his behavior was affecting her. What she wanted was to hear him describe how he had hurt her and express remorse, and this he said he couldn't do. They divorced.

Being willing to listen to your partner tell you how the lies and secrets affected her is valuable, but even more impacting is for you to tell her your perception – what you imagine the impact of your behavior has had on her life and how much you have hurt her. Your ability to validate her reality through your understanding of what you did to her, and then your willingness to say you were wrong and you are sorry are huge steps in demonstrating remorse. This is so important that it is useful to have a therapist guide you, but not everyone has access to therapists with experience in disclosure with addicts and their partners. A helpful alternative is to have a sponsor or other support person facilitate the disclosure. It is critical for your partner to have support afterward as well. Be prepared that she may not want that support to come from you. Offer anyway and have a backup. (Backup can be a friend who knows you have been having trouble, or someone she trusts who can hear what is happening and will offer your partner a safe haven to express her feelings and get away for a few hours or days.)

Not all partners want to know everything, especially partners who have been through many disclosures and are so angry or fragile they don't believe that they can hear anymore. This is true of partners of addicts who have relapsed numerous times. However, it is important to admit that you have relapsed before your partner discovers it. Our research clearly shows that in cases in which the addict discloses before the partner discovers a relapse, these couples report more satisfying relationships and more willingness by the partner to support the addict getting back into recovery.

If the disclosure is to your children, respect age-appropriate boundaries, and plan to explain the situation to them in ways that are meaningful for their developmental stage. Partners usually want to be a part of the process. (Disclosing to children will be discussed in the next chapter.)

Finally, you honor your own courage in being willing to come clean, and your partner's courage in being willing to listen. This process is in itself a hopeful sign for the future of your recovery and relationship.

Eight Steps to Disclosing with Integrity

Here are the steps to take in order to prepare and deliver a full disclosure in the form of an apology/amends letter:

1. **Get honest with yourself**. As the Fourth Step of AA says, "Made a searching and fearless moral inventory of ourselves." Making that inventory of how you have harmed another person and yourself with your behaviors helps raise your awareness about the extent of the damage. At the same time, recognize that those behaviors do not reflect your authentic, recovering self. Making a comprehensive inventory is not easy. You need to review your relationship from its beginning to the present, and list how you have been dishonest about how you felt about situations; how your feelings were displaced onto your family—for example, you were mean to your partner and the kids because you were angry at your mother or perhaps your boss; how you failed to set boundaries at work and became so stressed out that you made

bad decisions about your health and family finances; and how you have not honored or respected your partner or yourself through your continued lying. In this "working" document, include everything, not just addictive misconduct.

This usually takes some time, but it's important to take the time to do it. It also often brings up much guilt, shame, and pain. Sometimes when you are reviewing addictive behaviors or feeling shame you may be triggered to act out so as to escape from your feelings. To prevent a slip or relapse, first prepare a safety plan with your sponsor and/or someone to whom you can be accountable. Have several people on a call list that can be there for you when you are having a rough time, or ask another peer to be around when you are working on your list. Alert them before you start that you may be calling on them for help to get through your emotions or to get their feedback. Although you may be feeling shame, give yourself lots of positive self-talk for doing this important work.

2. With that information in mind, **write a draft of an "amends" or an "apology" letter**. (A sample of questions you might want to answer as part of information gathering for clarity Is located in the box below.) The first apology or letter of amends is a working document. This letter is not to be sent or read to your partner—it is a draft from which to be accountable with your higher power and/or your therapist or sponsor or someone you trust. In this letter be as detailed as you can about your behaviors that have been hurtful to others and yourself. Take full responsibility for what you have done. Do not blame others or try to excuse your behavior.

The following are useful questions to consider when writing your draft amends/apology letter:
1. If there was an affair, is it over? Are you still acting out in other ways? (If you still have strong feelings for this person, or have not yet determined you want to end this affair, you should address that with your therapist/sponsor before proceeding with formal disclosure. If you are not willing to give up the affair, then that is also what you have to disclose.)
2. Do you still have any contact with the person, or does your partner (i.e. was it a co-worker and your partner may still see that person at social functions)?

3. In what ways did the affair/problem behavior impact your relationship? What do you want to acknowledge about that in your letter to your partner?

4. Are there others for whom the affair/problem behavior is having or has had an impact on? (e.g. the partner or family of the person you acted out with, family members, co-workers, etc.)

5. What did the problem behavior solve or how did the behavior seem to make things better? What do you plan to do to manage those feelings in the future?

6. What lies were used to cover up your problematic behaviors?

7. Did your partner suspect, and if so, how much energy and additional lying was necessary to disarm your partner's suspicions? (For example, was the partner accused of imagining things, paranoia, etc. that perhaps contributed to the partner's anger or fear?)

8. Is this the only affair/behavior you have had, or has this been a recurrent pattern?

9. What impact is your problematic behavior still having on your relationship?

10. What would refusing to disclose mean for your recovery or your relationship?

11. What do you think will be the positive as well as negative consequences of revealing your problematic behavior (on your partner, on your relationship, on your children, friends, or family?)

3. Once you've finished writing the letter, **read it aloud to your therapist or ask a group of trusted recovering friends to hear it and then ask them for their reactions**. This feedback is often hard to hear, but rather than defend yourself, tolerate any negative feelings that come up by telling yourself that this is part of the process and that you have something to learn. Even if you disagree with what someone is saying, there is probably a bit of truth in what stings the most. Others can point out when you are minimizing your behavior. If they know you well enough, they may realize when you probably are omitting important information. Listen to them carefully and non-defensively. If they tell you that you need to redo the letter then do so and go back for a second reading. Stop only when they say you are ready to actually write your amends letter to read in person to your partner (or to whomever you are making a disclosure).

4. Now **write the letter as if you are going to read it to your partner**. You should state the goal of the letter in the very beginning. For example: "My goal in this letter is to be accountable for what I have done that has hurt you and the children/family/business. This letter

is written with all the honesty I can manage today [because if you are an addict of many years, you probably can't remember everything you have done]. Because of my actions, you may have been put in harm's way, and you deserve to have this information so you can make an informed decision about the future." [If she stays because she thinks she knows everything, but you continue to lie, then she is not staying of her own free will!]

We recommend that you DO NOT report all the "gory" details of your addictive behavior in this letter. For example, rather than telling the number of times you had sex, or the positions, or how good it was or wasn't, or the names of all the people you had sex with during your 10-year marriage, it is more useful to focus on the values you once had or wished you had. Admit that you broke the promises you made in your marital vows by having a number of affairs (or whatever the behavior has been) during your marriage. More importantly, admit you lied to her about the behaviors and be honest if you may have exposed her to health risks. This is also true if you have been using drugs and may have exposed your partner to Hepatitis C or HIV, have used family money for your drugs, have minimized your use, etc. If you've gambled away the children's college fund or there are going to be IRS ramifications because the taxes were not paid, this is important information for your partner to have. (If you have had an HIV test, bring the results with you when you are to read the letter and indicate that you have been tested and that you were wrong to subject her to this danger as much as you were wrong to have lied and engaged in the behaviors.) Tell her that you have not given specific details because you do not know how much she wants to hear, but are willing to answer any questions about your past behaviors as long as it is with the therapist or in an atmosphere where you both can get guidance about how to process and manage the information. Your intention is not to do further harm by disclosing. Yet you are committed to being transparent about your behaviors in the future after you have answered the questions she has.

You can also let her know what you have learned about yourself since you've gotten into therapy or recovery without blaming anyone else for your behavior. This is your opportunity to state that you have also hurt yourself because you have missed the opportunities to honestly love and be loved by her and your children. Reiterate that no matter what you have learned, you are responsible for your actions. If your intention is to stop these behaviors, say so here, but acknowledge that you understand there is no reason for her to believe you at this point. Again repeat that your actions have been wrong and hurtful and that you are sorry.

Once this letter is done, repeat the process outlined in Step 3 above. With feedback edit this letter to your partner until those helping you with this task tell you the letter is appropriate to share.

5. Arrange with your therapist or sponsor to **have two hours available to present the letter** to your partner. **Ask your partner to join you for a session with the therapist**. If she agrees, arrange with a friend to be on "standby" should your partner want you out of sight for a while. The friend needs to be someone who knows or can know about the disclosure and is willing not to know details beforehand but to be with your partner to be supportive.

6. **Practice** reading the letter, pray and/or ask others for help and guidance during this time.

7. Often partners already know about some of the behavior, but not all. Your partner may have written you a letter describing her anger and feelings about what she already knows or about the impact of your behavior on her. You may want to address information your partner provides in her letter in your disclosure. **With the guidance of your therapist, read the letter to your partner**. If you are with a sponsor, or by yourself, it is important that you preface the letter by stating that the information you will share may be hard to hear, but you feel it important to tell her. Have tissue available and some drinking water for both of you. Let yourself feel your feelings, and let your partner have and express her feelings, no matter how uncomfortable this may be for you. Regardless of her reaction, hang in there. If she calls you names, agree that you were wrong and she has every right to feel the way she does. Trust that you will do okay if you remain authentic.

8. Once reading the letter is complete, the therapist or sponsor should **ask your partner if she has any questions or wants to say anything to you**. Respond to those questions without getting defensive and support her expressing her feelings by telling her that she has every right to feel the way she does. Again repeat that you are willing to answer

any questions she may have in the future but you want the help of the therapist or sponsor/recovering couple. The therapist or sponsor then should ask if your partner is ready to accept the letter and the amends contained in it. Whether she says no or yes, **ask her what she needs now (today) to help the situation**. Then wait. Respond according to her request.

A Slightly Different Process

Another process that a colleague of ours uses combines the writing of a sexual history with writing your disclosure/amends letter. If you are in active therapy you might want to use your sexual history to help you write your disclosure/amends letter. Here is an example that uses a sexual history to help the partner understand what happened when:

Dear Barbara:

I appreciate that you came today, that you are listening to me, and how painful this is and will be for you. My goal today is to take responsibility for what I have done. This behavior started before we were married. In fact, it started when I was just entering puberty. I lied about it before we were married and I have lied throughout our marriage, but I am there to be honest now. I want you to know that you are not to blame for any part of my behavior. I am totally responsible for the choices I have made.

I will be specific later in this letter, but in general, as you know, I have repeatedly lied to you and attempted to make you feel like my actions were your fault. That is not the case – you did nothing to cause this. I put your health and our family's well being in danger; I have been selfish, uncaring, emotionally absent and not present for you or the kids. I engaged in risky behaviors and spent money that should have been used for you and our kids.

When I first met you in 1998, I was looking at porn on the Internet 3-4 times a week for at least 3 hours a day. You thought it was you and I did nothing to reassure you. I continued to look at porn and told you I wanted to wait to have sex with you because of my religious beliefs. You believed me and agreed. The truth was that my pornography use was increasing and by the time we got engaged I was viewing porn up to 6 or 7 hours a day, 4 or 5 times a week. We married in 1999 and I continued to lie to you and look at porn. At the time I was working for Jackson's and I started to stay late at work and began to go to chat rooms and engage in sexual talk with others. That is how the affairs started. I have met over three dozen women in the past ten years that I met online and have engaged in short-term affairs with them. I was not emotionally involved with them, just used the fantasy for masturbation and had unprotected sex with them when I could. Those were times when I would say I was working late, or had to be at a business meeting out of town over the weekend. At those times I did not want sex from you because I was exhausted from acting out. Again, that was not about you or your desirability. I was and am addicted. Although I was inappropriately angry and blamed you when you found the evidence of my most recent porn use and arrangements to meet the last woman, today I am grateful you cared enough to demand that I get treatment. Without that caring I would have just continued to take more risks and hurt you and our kids more. I am hopeful for the future since I have started down this road of recovery. I do not expect you to stay with me in this marriage. I do hope we can begin again. I am here to answer your questions and feel that telling you the truth is the first step for us to start over.

I love you more than you know – more than I ever knew.

Ben

The Timing and Extent of Formal Disclosure

In our survey, we asked addicts and partners for their recommendations regarding optimal timing of a formal disclosure. The results varied, often based on their personal experience. Many said as soon as possible.

After two years of recovery and both addict and partner working on a program, a partner advised:

Do it soon, and in the safety of a supportive environment, such as a therapist's office. Be fearlessly honest, but not detailed. Be willing to share without regard to consequences that might affect honesty. Try to understand your partner's feelings without judging them or closing down. Realize you are valuable and lovable, regardless of what anyone says or does. Look at being honest as a gift you give yourself. You can say, "That's who I really am." Give others the choice to decide to like you or not, to be with you or not.

We agree this is good advice.

Disclosure of Relapse

Not all partners want to know everything, especially partners who have been through many admissions and are so angry or fragile they don't believe that can hear anymore. This is true of partners of addicts who have relapsed numerous times. However, learning of your partner's relapse from him rather than by later discovering it is ultimately helpful for the relationship. Our research clearly shows that in cases in which the addict discloses before the partner discovers a relapse, these couples report more satisfying relationships and more willingness by the partner to support the addict getting back into recovery.

The next hardest disclosure is with children. Sometimes it is even harder than coming clean to your partner. Although it is difficult, disclosure to children is very important. How to do it depends on each child's circumstances and needs. The next chapter discusses how to explain things to children.

References

Burton-Nelson, Mariah. *The Unburdened Heart*. San Francisco: Harper, 2000.

Gottman, John. *The Science of Trust: Emotional Attunement for Couples*. New York: Norton, 2011.

Herman, Judith. *Trauma and Recovery: The Aftermath of Violence—From Domestic Abuse to Political Terror*. New York: Basic Books, 1992.

Chapter Six

What to Tell the Kids

Disclosing family secrets of all types to children is one of the most difficult tasks parents encounter. It may be harder for an addict to reveal his or her sexual acting out, drug use, or other addictive behavior to the child than to his partner. Addicts feel shame, anger, fear of alienating the children, fear that the children might be harmed by the information, and concern that they might tell others. All too often addicts think the solution has been simply to avoid sensitive subjects with children.

In describing families of sex addicts, Earle and Earle wrote in 1995:

> *"The secrets of parents cannot help but prove destructive to the child. No matter how deeply hidden or repressed by their parents, these secrets affect children. Secrets creep into every aspect of family living, creating high levels of psychological stress, pressure, and tension. The energy focused on keeping secrets does not allow children to be fully present. Children may not even be consciously aware of the family secrets, but these secrets seldom escape the unconscious."* (pg. 118)

People who are unwilling to share with their children often assume that the children did not know what was going on. In fact, children often know; research has shown that about two-thirds of children know about a parent's sexual acting out before disclosure, and even more when the parent has been using alcohol or other drugs. They may have overheard telephone calls, arguments, and conversations. They may have seen pornography on a parent's computer or iPhone, but may have kept the information to themselves. Even if they didn't know the details, they may have sensed the stress and tension between their parents.

Yet experts have tried to educate us for many years about the importance of appropriate sharing with children. Psychiatrist Carl

Jung wrote in 1969: "Telling children about your struggles helps them developmentally to have a realistic picture of what it means to be human." By telling older children about the addiction and recovery you can validate the children's feelings. Furthermore, it gives them permission to talk about what they may have felt and experienced during their parents' acting out.

It is important to note, however, that what we and others advocate is appropriate disclosure. Some partners blurt out information prematurely and in ways that blame the addict. They do this in order to get validation and support from their children, or as a means of expressing their anger at the addict and punishing him (or her). Such admissions often result in distancing the children from the addict, and partners who have done this usually subsequently regret it. In this chapter we will describe what an appropriate disclosure is.

Effects of a Parent's Addiction on the Children

A parent's addiction can have a major impact on the children. People who suffer from all varieties of addiction are consumed with planning, obtaining, using, or recovering from the use of their drug of choice. They then cover up their behavior and their shame and pain with lies and secrets. This behavior ignites the emotional distress of the partner. The partner understandably becomes obsessed with discovering evidence and catching the addict, reeling with anger and putting up emotional walls to stay detached, or pursuing with clingy behaviors. This behavior contributes to the emotional distress of the addict. Both parents mismanage the emotions that keep them trapped in addictive and sometimes codependent behaviors and intense shame. Often these parents are unavailable for the children emotionally and, at times, physically.

To compensate for their own insecurities and to reduce anxiety, addicted parents may engage in several different types of unhealthy behaviors with their children. They can be over-controlling, establishing rigid rules for children that are confusing and unrealistic. Addicted parents may use destructive criticism of the child to cover their own pain and shame. This shame sets up a family system with rigidly defined boundaries in which secrets are expected to be kept, rejection is common, people are self-focused, maturity is rarely modeled and underdeveloped, and everyone—parents and children—lacks a sense of security. Some children may attempt to solve parental problems by overachieving and being the "perfect" child, or by not rocking the boat in hopes of keeping the peace. Other kids take the opposite route— they are rebellious or engage in problematic behaviors to draw attention away from the parents' problems.

An 18-year-old boy, in treatment for marijuana and alcohol addiction, related:

> No matter what I did, it wasn't enough. I used to make the best grades, was captain of the swim team, even won a medal at a debate a couple of years ago. They didn't even notice, but if I make one B the shit hits the fan. So I figured what's the use? I'd just get high and see what they thought about that! That's when my drug use first started.

It is common for addicted people to have more than one significant relationship or marriage while they're using. Most single addicts, especially relationship addicts, become involved in serial relationships. Anxious for their children to accept their new partner, they bring this new person into the home soon after meeting him or her. If one or both members of the new couple are acting out sexually, the home environment is quickly sexualized. The couple may talk openly about the sexual desire for each other, touch each other in sexually explicit ways, or have little regard for the sexual sounds that can be overheard by children even through closed bedroom doors.

Sometimes the new partner is very attentive to the child. This can be very confusing for the child because of loyalty to the addict's former mate. The child may try to please the parent and becomes attached to the new partner, and then experiences another loss when the addicted parent moves on to yet another new partner.

Partners and addicts may make a child a confidant or even a surrogate spouse. These young people are given information and attention that are confusing and frequently far more sexualized or sophisticated than they can understand. Children hear and see the accusations and denials, the frightening fights, and the loud silence of stonewalling. Sometimes they see parents hit one another when anger gets mismanaged. Sometimes kids get hit as well.

Children may witness or find evidence of the drug use, gambling, or sexual acting out and are coerced to keep secrets about the addict's behavior with threats that to tell will result in the family breaking up or with Dad going to jail. Sometimes a child finds an Internet pornography file or emails from a sexual chat room on the home computer, or parent's iPad or Smartphone, and is faced with confronting the parent, telling the other parent, or holding onto the secret over time. When teens reach puberty, this secret-keeping can turn into intense rage and some teens even threaten to blackmail the addicted parent.

As discussed in previous chapters, some addicts act out in illegal ways and the disclosures happen through other sources such as police, attorneys, the spouse of an affair partner, or the media. The list is long and the potential for children to hear about the addictive behavior from other sources is greater than you might expect. Therefore, disclosure from you as the primary source is helpful to your relationship with the child. It is the first step in helping your children deal with the adverse consequences of other people's judgments and behaviors and their disappointment in you.

Contrary to what the media would have you believe, most children within a sexually addicted family are not overtly sexually abused. However, some are exposed to the sex addict's behaviors and use the behaviors as the seeds of their own sexual unfolding. Some adolescents and young adults find themselves caught up in sexual acting out and drug use that is similar to the ways the parent acted out.

Drug addicts sometimes use drugs in front of their children. Despite strict laws prohibiting adults from providing minors with illegal substances, some parents in addicted families even offer their kids drugs. It is common for addicts to reveal that their own parents smoked marijuana with them, or gave them alcohol at a very young age, or shared prescription medications. This modeling can send a mixed message about the inappropriateness and hazards of drug use or out-of-control behaviors by minors.

It is common for children in homes with eating disorders or out-of-control spending or gambling to watch an adult engage in destructive behavior. They often see the consequences and feel helpless to change things despite valiant efforts to do so.

My Dad always seemed lucky at cards and brought home lots of cash from the horse races. What I didn't know though was that he lost lots more, he just didn't bother to tell us. He used my college money to gamble with and lost. My grandmother gave me that money and it wasn't his. Mom told me that he had been betting on the horses on the Internet and now we have to pay back what he lost. Things are bad between them. If they just wouldn't fight maybe this would work out somehow. I hate it when they fight.

—17-year-old daughter of gambling addict

Any type of addictive behavior in a household is destructive to children, but making children the object of sexual acting out is one of the most problematic. Fear of abandonment or pain combined with the special attention of the parent makes this the perfect double bind for the child. While they fear the pain, they crave the attention and long to be special to the parent. It is common for adult survivors to describe how they feared and dreaded the sexual encounter with a parent, but at the same time how seductive was the pleasure of the attention and being told "you're special."

I'd stare at the door and hope it wouldn't open. When it did and he came over, I knew what to do, what he wanted. I hated the way he smelled, and can remember these sounds he'd make; when the sounds would start, I'd just go somewhere else [in my head] until I'd hear him say, "You're my girl, my best girl. I love you the most because you're special." As much as I hate him for what he did to me, I am ashamed to say I longed to see that look on his face the next day when he'd smile that smile—it was the only time I've ever felt like somebody. Later he told me he was addicted to me. I don't know what that means.

—20-year-old after leaving home, remembers abuse happening between ages 11 and 13

Because children are dependent on us, they feel they have few choices but to participate, often blaming themselves for what has happened. If they witness the abuse of another child, the guilt and pain are even more debilitating and long lasting.

When children's boundaries have been violated, especially by sexual abuse, they don't develop boundaries for anything. They often take on "protecting" someone else because they feel powerless to protect themselves. They don't recognize that their bodies are their own or that they have any say about what happens to them. They then become easy prey for someone else who has boundary issues themselves. It's not surprising that we see young people pairing up with unsuitable partners with whom they essentially repeat what happened to them in their family of origin.

Children raised in addicted families often have a variety of adverse experiences in childhood. We have touched on some of those categories in descriptions above. Specifically the Centers for Disease Control (CDC) categorize adverse experiences in childhood as: being victim of emotional, physical, or sexual abuse, living in an addicted household, living with someone who is chronically depressed or suicidal, or living in a household where the mother was treated with violence, a parent was incarcerated, separated or divorced. The CDC has well documented that there are enduring health and behavioral effects of childhood maltreatment (Anda, et al., 2005). These effects include an increase in substance abuse, early and impersonal sexual intercourse, greater than 50 sexual partners in a lifetime, increased use of nicotine, staying in relationships after they have become violent, post-traumatic stress reactions, and a host of physical problems including irritable bowel syndrome, unexplained panic, anxiety, and depression, and even increase in hypertension, and asthma. While this might scare you, it is important to realize that your children are affected in all sorts of ways because they live in an addicted household.

Addicted families are what Merle Fossum and Marilyn Mason, in *Facing Shame: Families in Recovery*, called shame-bound families. Their description provides an excellent overview of the dynamics of such families:

> *. . . A shame-bound family is a family with a self-sustaining, multi-generational system of interaction among a cast of characters who are (or were in their lifetime) loyal to a set of rules and injunctions demanding control, perfectionism, blame and denial. The pattern inhibits or defeats the development of authentic intimate relationships, promotes secrets and vague personal boundaries, unconsciously instills shame in the family members, as well as chaos in their lives and binds them to perpetuate the shame in themselves*

and their kin. It does so regardless of the good intentions, wishes, and love which may also be a part of the system.

In all cases of any kind of abuse, especially sexual abuse, the addict must be accountable for his actions, so some form of disclosure and acknowledgment is important for the child and the addict to heal. This is true even if the child is an adult by the time the addict gets enough recovery to take responsibility. The capacity of a parent to have a coherent and cohesive narrative about life's experiences and ability to reflect on and take responsibility for his or her behavior can actually interrupt the intergenerational transmission of psychopathology while building resilience in a child (Fonagy, et al., 1995, Siegel 1999).

To get in touch with the impact of your addiction on your child, think about or list ways your child has been exposed to addiction.

What do you think the impact this may have had on your child or evidence you already see of how this has impacted your child? In what ways was your child used?

How, What, and How Much Do We Tell

An impulsive disclosure to a child is yet another way children are impacted in negative ways as a result of addiction. Sometimes an addicted parent is forced to acknowledge behaviors because a child discovers the evidence, or another person tells or is going to tell part of the story (such as an angry or concerned partner, neighbor, relative, or information in the media) and it is important for the child to hear the truth from the addict in an age-appropriate way. Ideally a well-planned event with both parents involved, that has been reviewed and practiced in a therapeutic setting or with a sponsor, is the way to go. Unfortunately, that is not always possible.

Disclosure is best done after consideration of the following:

- When should we do this – soon after the addict tells the partner? Or do we wait until the addict has some recovery and/or the partner has calmed down?

- What do we do if it's on TV or in the newspaper?

- Who should be present – the addict alone, the partner alone, both? With the therapist?

- Should the kids be told together, or individually?

- What do children of various ages want or need to be told?

- How much do we reveal to the child?

- What information is private, just between the addict and partner, and what makes sense to talk to our kids about?

- How do we help our children be prepared for what others might say or ask?

In order to be able to give good advice to parents about whether or not to disclose, how much information to give, and what to expect after talking with the child, we conducted several surveys of sex addicts and partners who indeed had had to make decisions about if, when, and how to reveal to their children. Respondents reported a variety of circumstances, ranging from forced disclosure (because of arrest, threats by others to reveal, or insistence by the partner), to a well-planned event in a therapeutic environment. Below are a few examples from parents who participated in our past research published in an article (Corley & Schneider, 2003). The first is of a disclosure done very early, and by the partner alone, without the addict's participation or presence. She disclosed to both of her children, but spoke to each one at a time in an age-appropriate manner.

> *Within one month after discovery of my husband's behaviors, I told my older son, who was 11 at the time, that his father was addicted to pornography and that it was harmful to our relationship because pornography objectifies women. I told him about it at home without anyone else present. I told my daughter, who was 7 that we were having problems, that Daddy and Mommy needed help, and that we were getting it. My son was tearful and scared, afraid we would separate. He was able to ask me questions about sex, pornography, and addiction. My daughter tried to cheer everyone else up, a budding codependent, but later was able to discuss her feelings of fear. I told the children different things because I thought the little one was too young to understand, but I talked to her about it when she turned 10. My son apparently blocked out the disclosure of his father's sexual addiction, and three years later claimed he didn't know about it.*

An addicted and convicted sex offender wrote,

> *I think it depends on the addict's own recovery progress and the age of the children. If the addict is staying sober and is motivated to recover, and the kids are at a minimum teenagers, it's the right time. If the public is notified of a sex offender, the addict should disclose before the public is informed. The child should hear about the offending behavior from the parent and not through other sources.*

When disclosure is a choice, the positive reasons for doing so include validating what the child already knows, divulging before others tell, in hope of breaking the cycle of addiction, and for the child's safety (Black et al, 2003). Unfortunately, some explanations to children are impulsively given by partners who want to punish the errant addict or who want the children to side with them rather than the addict. Others are forced by circumstances, such as public disclosure, and the parents have very little time to reflect on their fears or concerns. Here is an account of the experience of a 17-year old boy whose father was a federal judge:

> *My Dad beat up this drug dealer who was with a prostitute and he was arrested. That's how my Mom found out that he was a sex addict and a drug addict. Then he talked to me and my sister. That went okay. I was really mad at first, but my Dad seemed so changed after he went to treatment that it was good. It really prepared us for what was about to happen. He's a big shot in our town—or at least he was until this happened. When he went to court, the newspapers and TV stations got word of his deal and they printed this trash about him in the paper—it was even on the TV news. My folks knew it was going to happen and we all got together and decided what we were going to say to people. The news media got the old "no comment" line like you see on TV, but with friends it was hard. Everybody was tweeting about it, saying really horrible things about my Dad and some about me. At first I was really embarrassed but then some of my friends were really cool and supported me against some other freaks at school. It isn't such a big deal now. I am proud about how we all got through it.*

Children's Reactions to Disclosure (Parents' description)

Before describing how best to disclose to children, we would like to relate the parents' perception of how children react. Most children's initial reactions to revelations of a parent's sexual acting, drug use, or gambling are perceived as negative. Usually children are shocked and in disbelief; some say the information validates their suspicions or actual knowledge. This turns to fear and sadness because they are worried that their parents will separate or divorce and are concerned about what will happen to them. Many older children express anger towards the addict and try to support the partner; often they voice anger about the impact on their lives. Sometimes this results in their own acting out in dangerous or addictive ways or anxious attempts to cheer everyone up or comfort one or both parents. Occasionally a child will praise the addict for getting help or the couple for appearing to work together to solve problems. Although at the time of disclosure some children appeared to understand, months or years later they were surprised when told again. This is more likely to be true of younger children.

Below are some examples of what parents reported to us. This mother of older children described the aftermath of a disclosure that was forced by a young adult's suspicions. It resulted in the entire family getting into treatment. Premature disclosure by the addict led to additional traumatic events, but eventually the family adjusted.

My young adult daughter became increasingly suspicious and began asking questions. When she and I were alone in the car one day, she asked me outright if Dad had had affairs, and I answered yes. This was the catalyst to us getting into recovery. Two months later, my 22-year old son noticed some Twelve-Step books lying around and asked questions. We set up an appointment with our therapist to have a controlled disclosure, but then my husband inappropriately pulled him aside and dumped it on him when they were alone in a car. My 13-year old son was told soon thereafter in a planned disclosure by his father in the therapist's office with the entire family present.

My daughter's reaction was anger and tears. She wanted more information. She needed lots of time and emotion for weeks and weeks. She wouldn't talk to [her] dad – she wanted to be with me all the time. My 22-year old son told his father he didn't want any more information, but he wanted me to tell him more. Two days later my husband missed an important family appointment, and in response my son slit his wrist. It was a major event – ambulance, emergency room. . . When my 13-year old son was told, he cried, and said, "It feels like my family is falling apart." He asked no questions.

Now we are open at home and my son hears talk about addiction and about our counseling and Twelve-Step groups. I often ask him if he has questions, and he always says no. My older children ask me specific questions about the addiction and broad questions about how their dad is doing. My husband is still not open and comfortable talking with the kids, but they do both speak with him about Twelve-Step groups.

A 55-year -year old physician, whose acting out had included internet pornography and prostitution, disclosed to his 3 children, ages 10-19 years old, a short time after telling his wife, who then asked him to leave. The disclosure took place in the home, with all family members present.

I told them I had violated my wife's trust and that we would be separating. I told them I would be in therapy to resolve the problem. Only the youngest said anything. On the verge of tears, he asked how long I would be gone. They were otherwise shocked and speechless.

Timing of Disclosure to Children

It is surprising how many parents do not disclose to their children, despite awareness of the value of doing so. Most parents choose not to tell, delay telling, or disclose with trepidation. The addicts in our study had four primary concerns that fueled their decision not to tell. The main concern was fear of loss of the relationship with the partner or child. Early on in recovery, the partner is fragile and these addicts wanted her to gain more recovery before divulging difficult material. This was especially true when the addicted person needed to acknowledge that he had acted out with men as part of his addiction or had determined he was gay. Partners said they postponed disclosure until they were not so angry and wanted evidence that the addict was serious about his or her recovery.

Some addicts feared the partner might use the information in a custody battle. This is a legitimate concern – we have seen several cases in which the information used in a disclosure was then used against the addict in custody hearings. However, if a disclosure is well planned, often the results are that the child actually sees that the addict is taking responsibility for his or her action.

Some addicts and partners reported that they felt the child was too young to understand or that the child was so out of control with his or her own behavior, the parents did not want to add fuel to the fire.

All these reasons are important. If you are fortunate enough to have escaped forced or impulsive disclosure, so that you have an opportunity to work through the above factors, both of you can benefit from discussing them with a therapist and planning the timing and content of the event so as to minimize the adverse consequences. Our research and clinical experience concludes that it depends on the circumstances of your situation. Both partners and addicts agree that is it important that both of them are working on their own issues as well as working together on some level as co-parents. At the same time, it's important not to wait too long because the children already can see and feel that something is wrong. It's a good thing to say that as a couple you are having some problems but are trying to work on those problems, and that none of what is going on is the fault of the children.

What Kids Want to Know

After hearing an apology letter read to him in a disclosure session with his parents and the therapist, a 15-year-old boy related:

> My Dad and Mom asked me to talk to them. My Dad said he had done some things wrong and needed to talk to me about that. He read me a letter and said he was a sex addict. We had talked about addiction at school and sex addiction was mentioned but I really didn't know what that was. He told me he'd lied to Mom and to us kids and that he was wrong to do that. He had gotten involved with other women and spent lots of time looking at pornography like people drink or use drugs, instead of figuring out how to solve his

problems. He says that is why he goes to meetings, so he can learn to solve his problems. He apologized for leaving his porn where I could see it and said that it was a bad thing to look at pictures of women and make them into objects. Things like that. He said he was sorry that he had been gone all the time and that he hadn't made it to my baseball games or track meets.

I guess what I remember most is that he said he was sorry, that it was wrong to lie and that he loved me and he would try to do better. I believe him.

That was an example of a disclosure well done.

Based on our studies and clinical experience we know it is not necessary to disclose to very young children. They may understand the concept of lying or breaking a promise, but the concept of addiction is beyond their cognitive ability. Below is a list of suggestions about what kids want to know, by age:

Pre-school, ages 3-5

These children have often been witness to fighting or have heard that you are an addict and don't know what is happening. They want to know:

- Are you going to die or leave me?

- Am I in trouble?

- Do you love me?

- Do I have to do something to fix this?

They need guidelines and structure about their behavior and reassurance none of this is their fault or their responsibility to fix. This is when consistency counts from you. Because you have been out-of-control doesn't mean they get to be out-of-control (this is true for all the age groups). When their confusion results in tantrums or rule breaking for attention, connect with them and then redirect their behavior. (Too often sex-addicted families get hypervigilant and worry about a child's normal sexual exploration and genital stimulation. See Debra Haffner's *From Diapers to Dating* for excellent information about what is normal.)

<u>Early Elementary (ages 5–6)</u>

- Is this my fault?

- Will something bad happen? (divorce fear)

- Who are you now? You are now very different and this child has learned to adapt to deprivation.

They need encouragement to talk about how they feel and reassurance that none of what is happening is their fault. Drawing pictures and then talking is good way to get the conversation going. Some children fall back on best behaviors in hopes that if you divorce they are not abandoned. It is important to let them know exactly when you will be with them and then to follow through.

<u>Upper elementary/middle school (9–13)</u>

- Am I normal?

- Will I get this addiction because I have sexual feelings?

- Am I going to end up a drug addict because you are?

- What will happen to me if you get divorced?

Pre-teens are concerned about being normal anyway, so dealing with the addiction adds to those worries. Helping them with facts about changes in their bodies and brains of this stage in life can give reassurance. It is also helpful to explain that addiction is an unhealthy way to cope with emotional distress, and that you need to learn together other ways to cope when either of you is upset. If separation or a divorce is likely, be honest that it is a possibility but that no firm decision has been made until you and your partner have had time to figure things out; emphasize that no matter what happens, you will still be their dad or mom and will always love them.

<u>Teen/Adult years</u>

- How could you do this to Mom? To the family?

- How does this specifically relate to me? (You've ruined my life!)=

Listen to the feelings of your teen or grown children. Ask questions about their fear or anger. Seek to understand and stay connected. It is important to reinforce or clarify family rules even if you have been a rule breaker in the past, your job is still to be the parent in the present.

In contrast to the above list, here are the things that kids don't want to know:

- The specific details of your acting out

- How angry you are at your spouse

- How sex is between you and your spouse or anyone else

Generally, small children do not need disclosure or explanation about addiction. An apology for not being around is appropriate, but mostly they need good parenting. Older children can benefit from information about sex addiction and addiction in general. There is some genetic predisposition for addiction. Because you are an addict, your children are likely to have an increased risk; therefore, discussing your addiction with older children is appropriate and disclosure is one way to do this.

Because children of different ages need different types of information, you need to consider this when planning your disclosure. If your children's ages aren't close together, it is probably best to disclose separately to each one. And of course, in such cases you need to take into account how to give an older child information that you want him or her to keep private from the younger child until the younger child is mature enough to hear additional information. None of this is easy.

What and how much to tell becomes the challenge. And how can you be both accountable and a good parent? There are no perfect answers for how you tell kids or what you divulge. We are going to recommend a process instead of telling you all the "right" things to say. We will give you some concrete examples, but this disclosure has to fit your situation.

First and foremost, your job as a good parent is to make your love visible by providing structure, guidance, protection, and nurturing in healthy ways. It is to help your child integrate the feelings about what has happened to her during your addiction with her thoughts and help her plan future actions about her feelings. This is a difficult task since most addicts had little or no modeling from their parents on these topics. If this is true for you, you may need to do some homework.

Figuring this out starts with a foundation—a foundation made up of your values and then learning some new skills

It also means getting rid of faulty core beliefs. That takes time and requires taking active steps to change how you think, which changes how you feel, and in turn increases your chances of changing what you do. Most addicts have a set of negative beliefs about self that need to be corrected to a set of hopeful, positive beliefs that people in recovery utilize. A sample of negative core beliefs outlined in *Out of the Shadows* by Patrick Carnes are representative of what many addicts report as fueling their distorted thinking and destructive values.

- I am basically a bad, unworthy person.

- No one would love me as I am.

- My needs are never going to be met if I have to depend on others.

- Sex (alcohol, drugs, food, gambling) is my most important need.

Think about how your core beliefs have influenced your value system. Perhaps you are not sure what your values are or you may want to change or improve your values. Here are a few questions to get you started.

- Where did you get your values? Parents? Other family members? Teachers? Preachers/Rabbis/Leaders in the faith community you were raised in?

- Which values that you learned in childhood can serve you well now?

- Are there values you learned that are not respectful of your personal growth or recovery? What faulty beliefs were generated from those messages?

- How would you change or adapt both the beliefs and values to better suit you as a strong person in recovery who is also a responsible parent?

- Review your values with your partner/co-parent. Together list the values you both want to guide you in creating structure, guidance, protection, and nurturing for your children (and yourselves!).

It is important for you to take responsibility for your actions, but not to condemn yourself over and over. It will be helpful for you to list statements that counter or refute those negative core beliefs above. Let this new set of values help you develop positive counter statements.

Your values as a person in recovery and new core beliefs that reflect those values can make everything easier if you actually follow them. It is much easier to disclose when you start out by admitting that you violated a value and that you had a faulty belief. For example, think about your behavior in the past. What were the values that guided that behavior? What values do you want to guide you now?

Here is a sample of what you might say to a teenager just about honesty and being faithful:

> When I was growing up, I heard a lot about being honest and faithful in relationships. Yet, I did not see much of that, and my own experience led me to think I could get away with lying and feel powerful if I had lots of girlfriends. But I was mostly lying to myself. When I think about it, I was lonely and was faking it and that is what I have been doing for a long time. For years I have been telling lies to Mom, to you, and to myself—and that has hurt everyone. Because I have lied, Mom doesn't trust me and she has every right to be mad. What I did was wrong—lying to her and to you was wrong and I am sorry that I have lied.
>
> Lying is easier to talk about than being unfaithful because I am ashamed of what I have done. When I should have been with your Mom and you, I chose to find some other women to be with when I felt mad, or sad, or lonely, and some of the time I had sex with them. This was very hurtful to your Mom, to our relationship and to the family—including you. It will take your Mom a long time to start trusting me again and she has every right to be mad at me. You did not do anything to make me do this. None of this is your fault or Moms. I made wrong choices myself.

For a younger child, you might say:

> Your Mom and I have been fighting because I have been telling lies to her. Because I have lied, Mom doesn't trust me and she has every right to be mad. What I did was wrong—lying to her was wrong. Sometimes I even lied to you about working when I was off doing

stuff with people I should not have been with. When I should have been with your Mom and you, I chose to find some other people to be with when I felt mad, or sad, or lonely. Sometimes I would drink and do things that were dangerous and then lie to Mom about what I was doing when she was worried about me. Now I go to meetings at night to learn better ways to make decisions when I am feeling sad, or mad. What I did was very hurtful to your Mom and to our family—including you. It will take your Mom a long time to start trusting me again and she has every right to be mad at me. You did not do anything wrong. Neither did Mommy. I was the one who did things that were wrong. I am sorry I hurt her and that I have not been around much to spend time with you. I love you.

There is something very empowering about being honest.

Let's look at how this fits our previous discussions of parenting in terms of structure, guidance, protection, and nurturing. Think about marriage or a committed relationship. You might list your values about being in a marriage. You might want to write the messages you want to send to your children to guide them about marriage and commitment in what you say and do.

It is common to feel guilty about what you have done in your addiction and to try to overcompensate by letting children run all over you. This is especially true when they reach their teen years and will use your addiction history to manipulate you. But your job as a parent is to provide structure to protect your child. Sometimes you have to be firm and you might say,

I can see that you don't think it's fair that you are not allowed to "hook up" (or date) now, and that you think that because I was irresponsible when I was in my addiction, I should let you do dangerous things now. But my irresponsibility hurt others as well as myself. The rule in our house is that children do not drive cars or go to parties or get-togethers without an adult chaperone until they are 16 because we value your life. Since it is our job to protect you the best we can, and the odds are greater that you will get hurt if you drive or party with friends at this early age without a parent supervising, you will have to wait until you are older and have more experience with life. Since you are 14 and have acted pretty mature at times, we agree that we will talk about when you can go with a

group to an event without us, but for now—no "hooking up" or dat-
ing alone. I see that you are angry and that's normal when someone
is hoping to do something special and it has to be postponed. It's
okay to be angry and we have talked about ways to deal with anger
in the past. I have confidence in you and think you will get beyond
the anger and decide how you want to be with your friends in ways
that fit our values and rules.

Certainly some 14 year olds will ignore this and do it anyway. But if they know your values, the rules, and the reasons behind them, it is more likely than not they will follow your rule. It is also valuable to give your kids a way out; sometimes kids don't want to do something that a peer is pressuring them to do. By co-creating a code sentence or phrase so when they call and use that phrase you know it means that they need to be picked up or that they want you to say no to a request.

Nurturance means that you take time out to spend with your children. No matter how old kids are, they need to know they have some special time with you as an adult, as somebody who loves and cares about them and listens. If you go to the movies with your children but rarely have any one-on-one time to talk and listen to each other, time with your children is not as valuable as it could be. Going to the movies together is better than nothing at all, but taking time to talk about what is going on in their lives and how they feel is important for people to feel valued.

Feeling valued translates into healthy families. Mark Laaser contrasts unhealthy and healthy families in his book *Healing the Wounds of Sexual Addiction*. As you review the characteristics of healthy and unhealthy families in the next paragraph, think about the values you were raised with and have operated with as an addict and see what you want to change.

In unhealthy families boundaries are either very rigid or nonexistent. In healthy families boundaries are firm but flexible. Parents care and nurture each other and their children. There is personal respect for boundaries. In unhealthy families, the rules are centered on keeping the secret, so people are not to acknowledge what is going on. It is the "don't ask, don't tell" rule so you just don't talk. With that rule comes the injunction not to feel anything, to blame others for your problems, to minimize and deny that problems even exist unless it will get you something. Children in these families take on roles that are rigid and defined.

In healthy families, children's roles are more flexible, but the parents stay in the adult position so children have a chance to grow and mature over time. People take personal responsibility for their actions, and honesty is rewarded. People talk and feel, and accept that problems are inevitable in life and can be dealt with, and these folks can ask for help. People listen to each other, individuality and teamwork are both supported and encouraged, and feelings are accepted. Physical self-care is modeled and taught, children feel safe and know that they can always come home. Basic needs are provided for. Healthy families learn to cope with and express a full range of emotions. Spirituality plays an important role in daily living.

How to Help Your Child Do Well

As shown in some research in the area of prevention education, some basic characteristics are consistently seen in children who do well in the world. These can help you shape your parenting plan. Children who are successful as adults (and during childhood) have high emotional intelligence. Daniel Goleman, author of *Emotional Intelligence,* describes people with high emotional IQ as having five specific abilities:

1. The ability to recognize a feeling when it happens

2. The ability to handle feelings in appropriate or self-enhancing ways

3. The ability to motivate self to delay gratification and stifle impulses

4. The ability to recognize emotional states of others (having empathy)

5. The ability to respond rather than react to emotional states of others

Researchers are finding that these skills can be taught to children (and adults), who then improve in many areas of their lives. In fact, children who have good impulse control (#3) are less likely to become addicts. It makes sense when you think about how addicts are so impulsive with their actions.

Daniel Siegel, a researcher and psychiatrist, has written many books about the brain and how to help children learn to use both sides of their brains so as to have better emotional intelligence. In his book, *The Whole Brain Child* (2011), he talks about the importance of helping your child use all parts of his brain to deal with emotional situations. He points out that the brain has specific parts that have specific jobs. The left side of the brain helps you organize thoughts and think logically, while the right side helps you experience emotions and read other people's non-verbal communications. He also reminds us that we have an old brain – some people talk about this as the reptilian brain – and he tells children that this is our downstairs brain which jumps into action in emergencies to help us be ready to fight, flee, or freeze in a split second. Our newer brain region, or what he calls the upstairs brain, helps us make moral and ethical decisions. When we use our whole brain, we help these parts work together. He outlines ways in which you can help your kids to integrate information and emotions.

For example, let's say your daughter is very upset about the rules you have set for bedtime and the subject matter she can watch on TV. Tonight her focus is on not being allowed to watch an episode of a series on TV that everyone has been talking about. You have told her once that she is late for bed time, she continues to postpone going to bed, and is now whining in the doorway.

Instead of using the command and demand strategy that most of us were raised on, there is another way. First, it is important to connect with your child when she is upset. Sit or kneel down to her eye level and rub her shoulder or her back in circle, close to where the heart is located. Look into her eyes and using a nurturing calm voice say something like "Gosh, you sound upset." While still rubbing, with neutral expression say, "Sometimes it is just hard to get through tough times isn't it?" Reassure her : "I want you to know I love you very much and you are so special. Can you tell me what is going on?" Repeat what she says is the problem, then redirect or offer more reassurance if she moves toward doing the right thing.

This strategy of "reconnect and redirect" allows you to use both your right brain to sense what is going on emotionally with your daughter (sad, mad, fearful, confused, frustrated, etc.) and provide right brain soothing by safe body contact of rubbing her back in circles around her heart. By hearing her feelings and how she is experiencing the distressful situation, you also reinforce that she is important to you. Through redirection if she is engaging in behaviors that are making things worse, depending on her age you can co-create a solution for what to do next.

Sometimes all it takes to relieve some of that distress is for her to feel heard and important to you. At other times, it takes more attention to the situation and your using the left side of your brain – that logical side – to think through suggestions to help. And that is the second strategy – to *redirect with the left,* so that instead of ignoring or using a harsh tone, you are thinking through what she needs to feel safe and secure so that she can get through the disappointment of not getting her way, while also abiding by the family's rules that are now based on healthy values.

Not all children know what they are feeling – probably like you. If you are in therapy, most likely you are often asked how something makes you feel. It is important to learn about the basic emotions we are all born with. Interest, excitement, joy and enjoyment are the feel-good ones – our body actually feels good when we experience them. Other emotions (startle, fear, distress, anger, disgust, confusion, shame, humiliation) don't feel so good physically. In fact, the body may give us a cue when that emotion is present. For example, when you get angry, your blood pressure may go up, heart rate rises, jaw may be tight and your stomach churns. The more you know about how you are feeling, the more you can make good decisions about what to do that will help the situation. For kids, Siegel and Goleman remind us to name the emotion and talk about how it feels in the body in order to tame it. Siegel recommends using story-telling as a way to calm distressing emotions (or to celebrate the good feeling ones). If you have little children, concepts like the right and left side of the brain are too difficult to comprehend, but grade school and older children understand that the right side of the brain is where our feelings get going, the left brain can help us put feelings into words, and they two sides can work together to help us plan what to do at the moment or in the future.

Another characteristic found in youngsters who do well is the ability to set reachable goals. Additionally, these children feel that they know who they are—they have a sense of self-worth and self-identity. These young people are able to talk to their parents about anything (including sex) and talk with them often. In fact, talking is encouraged in these families and the family members report feeling heard.

Finally these children know their family's values and can articulate them. Think about how much easier it is for a kid to set boundaries with other children when he knows why you value boundaries and he has practiced with you how to set and keep a boundary.

Because we are speaking about sexual issues, it is also important to mention what happens in sexually healthy families. Parents consider sexuality education as important as all other types of values-based education. Parents are "askable"—children feel safe in asking. Parents utilize "teachable" moments rather than waiting for children to ask questions. They are aware that actions speak louder than words. Parents in these families know the difference between childhood and adult sexuality. Are you prepared to do these things?

Children in sexually healthy families feel good about their bodies, and understand the concept of privacy with regard to boundaries. They are prepared for puberty and feel comfortable asking their parents questions. They are able to make age-appropriate decisions.

So what does this have to do with disclosing to your children? This forms the foundation by which you will continue to talk about sexuality in your family. Disclosure to children means assuming responsibility for how your sexual acting out, drug abuse or addiction, compulsive gambling or other addictions, or your codependent behaviors have interfered with parenting your children. The discussions that follow are critical to rebuilding family and to helping your child grow up thinking in a healthier way than you did about sexual and other behaviors.

Basic Repair Work

In preparing to disclose, here is what you need to do:

1. Think about what you want to say about the values you violated by your acting out rather than the details of what you did. In other

words, how you failed your child is what you want to be accountable for. Your child is not interested in how many affairs you had or how much money you lost. He is interested in the fact that you lied to him, that you are sorry about it, and that he did not do anything to cause this. It is important to admit that you lied to his mother many times and lost her trust and that she will probably be angry and sad about it for a while, but that it is normal for her to feel that way. It makes sense that she'd be angry and that your child too would be angry that you lied. He might remember that you are serious when you admit that you spent money on things you did not need and that the money should have gone into his college fund or something for the family and you were selfish and for that you are sorry. Take some time and list those values you violated when you were using.

2. Discuss with your partner what information you both think needs to remain private between you as adults and marriage partners. (Some information may be okay for adult children to hear.) If it is not information that is crucial for children in order to make sound decisions about their own lives, then it can remain private between the two of you. Discuss with your mate the differences between the old values you were living by and the new ones that are driving your decisions now. Make a list of those together so you are both working from same value system.

4. Prepare to admit where you made mistakes and encourage your child to talk about how she feels about what you've said. (To keep the communication flowing, let your child know that she can think about it, write you a letter, or draw you a picture about how she is feeling.)

5. If you are using the letter format, write it now. Sometimes, with younger children, people have made picture stories to tell the "story." (Age- appropriate language and format should be remembered in the preparation.) Others have made digital videos, especially if the addict is unable to disclose in person to the child. These formats are good since each allows the child to have something he can hold onto, review, think about, and then respond to. The document or video is a hopeful "security blanket" for getting a new parent back for the child, so it should be a good incentive for you to stay in recovery to honor this rebuilding with your child.

6. You should read the letter or tell the story to your child. Both parents should be present and in agreement about what is going to be shared. Because it is a highly emotionally charged time for most people, it is safer for children to see both parents being involved in the process. *But the addict is responsible for disclosing his behavior.* (Partners often are aware that at times their behavior has been hurtful to the children too. The same process works, just at a different time.)

7. Ask your child what she has heard or already knows and if she has any questions.

8. Remind him that he is free to ask you questions, and that you understand that this is hard for some people to talk about, so you are going to bring it up again from time to time.

Other Ongoing Repair Work

- Look for moments that are teachable opportunities—for example, a cybersex story on TV, cigarette use by young people or adults in a movie, or when someone gets arrested for prostitution.

- Focus more on the positive part of recovery—everyone working to have a balanced life.

- Spend time doing fun things together to balance the "heavy" conversations you're having with your children. Children (especially early in your recovery) need fun time, too.

- If your child is angry and wants time apart from you, give him some space. However, do not forget the job of a parent is to provide structure and guidance. Encouraging your child to write you a letter about his anger is appropriate. Letting him hit you or allowing him to ignore house rules just because you didn't follow them is not okay. If the anger persists, and "connect and redirect" aren't working, then family therapy is in order.

- Discuss more about healthy sexuality other rather than just rehashing the old information about the disclosure.

- Be available. Be patient. Be proud that you are making every effort to be a different kind of parent. It will be worth it.

Despite the problems between you, you and your partner will want to show your children a united front in the fight against addiction in the way you disclose to them and in discussions after the disclosure. If they see you together even though the addict has misbehaved, it can help them to feel less anxious about the future and your role with them.

If a separation or divorce is the best solution for you, then co-parent your children in ways that show them that people can end one type of relationship and transition to another respectfully. When parents end up separating, the losses for children are multiple, so their needs are compounded by grief, fear, anger, and sadness.

Disclosure is not just a matter of having one little talk and it's over. In our most recent research on relapse, the majority of those respondents unfortunately had not yet disclosed to their children. Adult children tell us it is a very important part of the healing process for them as well. Let the disclosure start an ongoing process requiring many discussions.

There will be many opportunities for you to have teachable moments, so brainstorm with others what you will do and say when issues come up with your children. Think through what you will do if you find your daughter on the Internet chatting with some guy several years older than she and you find out it is she who is trying to talk him into meeting for sex. Or what you will do if you find printed pornography, pornography saved, or sites visited on your child's computer or phone, or if you walk into your twelve-year-old's room with a stack of laundry and find him or her masturbating. Or how you will handle watching a television program with your seven-year-old if a female character makes a sexually aggressive comment to a male. Yes, disclosure is but the first of many opportunities to talk about sexual health, drug use and abuse, healthy relationships, and developing into a responsible, authentic person. Your job is to keep coming back, offering to talk, listening, writing notes, being there for serious and fun times—but be there. Children of all ages need parental involvement and supervision. Be as genuine as possible. Don't lose your sense of humor. Have integrity about what you say and do with your children and you can survive almost anything.

Disclosure and discussing addiction are serious business, so limit the time you spend talking about the disease and expand the time you spend with your children talking about what they want to discuss, having fun, and having a positive attitude about the future.

References

Anda, Robert et al. The enduring effects of abuse and related adverse experiences in childhood. *European Archives of Psychiatry & Clinical Neuroscience*, 2006.

Carnes, Patrick. *The Betrayal Bond: Breaking Free of Exploitive Relationships*. Deerfield Beach, Fla.: Health Communications, Inc, 1997.

Carnes, Patrick. *Out of the Shadows*. New York: Bantam, 1991.

Corley, M. Deborah and Schneider, Jennifer. Sex addiction disclosure to children: The parents' perspective. *Sexual Addiction & Compulsivity*, 10: 291-324, 2003.

Corley, M. D., Schneider, J. P., & Hook, J. N. (in press). Partner Reactions to Disclosure of Relapse by Self-Identified Sexual Addicts. *Sexual Addiction and Compulsivity*.

Earle, Ralph & Earle. Marcus. *Sex addiction: Case studies and management*. New York: Brunner Mazel. (1995)

Fongay, P. et al. Attachment, borderline states and the representation of emotion and cognition in self and other. In D. Cicchetti, S. L Toth, et al. (Eds.), *Emotions, cognition, and presentation* (pp. 371–414). Rochester, NY: University of Rochester Press, 1995.

Fossum, Merle & Marilyn Mason. *Facing Shame: Families in Recovery*. New York: Norton, 1986.

Goleman, Daniel. *Emotional Intelligence*. New York: Bantam, 2006.

Haffner, Debra. *From Diapers to Dating: A Parent's Guide to Raising Sexually Healthy Children*. New York: Newmarket Press, 1999.

Laaser, Mark.*Healing the Wounds of Sexual Addiction*. Grand Rapids, Mich.: Zondervan Publishing, 2004.

Siegel, Daniel. *The Developing Mind: Toward a Neurobiology of Interpersonal Experience*. New York: Guilford Press. (1999).

Siegel, Daniel. *The Whole-Brain Child: Revolutionary Strategies to Nurture Your Child's Developing Mind*. New York: Delacorte Press. 2011.

Chapter Seven
The Other Disclosures

Previous chapters have described secrets, lies, and the initial disclosures involving interactions between a married or committed couple. But this is not the only kind of secret keeping that you may have to face. This chapter describes several real-life situations in which people have to decide whether to keep information private and hold a secret or to reveal it, and, if the latter, to whom. Let's begin with the story of the Malik family –Michael, his wife Martha, and their daughter Marjorie. Michael's cybersex addiction affected his entire family:

Michael, a 38-year old married computer programmer, had a long history of compulsive masturbation. A crisis ensued early after he had spent too much money on pornographic magazines. He had thrown out the collection and promised his wife Martha to reform. Since then, he'd still masturbated frequently and had a small stash of porn pictures, but he managed to keep the situation under control. Martha suspected that Michael's habit had not disappeared, and kept an eye out for pornography in their home.

Within months after Michael discovered the Internet, however, his addiction was again in full swing. He spent hours holed up in his study at night viewing online pornography, engaged in sex talk with other women in chat rooms, and eventually having real-time sex with women online using video streaming. Of course, he kept all of this a secret from Martha. Michael was thrilled that with cybersex, the secret was easier to keep because there was no longer a paper trail. Martha knew that Michael's interest in sex with her had diminished, but he explained that it was because he was working so hard and was too tired.

Late one evening, thirteen-year-old Marjorie walked into her father's study without knocking and found him masturbating while his digital camera transmitted pictures of him to someone at the other end of the computer screen. Appalled, she yelled that she was going to get her mother. Michael quickly collected himself, rearranged his clothing, flipped off the computer screen, and begged Marjorie to first talk with him. He reminded Marjorie of how depressed her mother had been recently. He assured her that he hadn't really had sex with another person, and implored her to keep the secret, for to tell would only hurt Martha. He told Marjorie that revealing the secret might result in breakup of the family, or even in a suicide attempt by Martha. In the end, he swore her to secrecy and promised to stop the behavior.

As we mentioned in Chapter 6, a situation like this puts the child in an impossible loyalty conflict for which there seems to be no way out. It guarantees that the child will feel guilty towards the unknowing parent. Her relationship with her father and siblings will also be altered – she is now in a position to blackmail her father in various ways and will also now feel a barrier between herself and her siblings, from whom she also has to keep the secret. To ask a child to hold a major secret from a parent is to do the child a grave disservice.

Learning about a person's sexual secrets from a child – or for that matter from any other source than the person – without a doubt increases the betrayal that a partner feels. If you recognize that you are about to be "outed," your best defense is to arrange to promptly disclose your secret yourself. Recalling the story of the Malik family at the beginning of this chapter, Michael's effort to persuade his daughter Marjorie to collude with him in keeping the secret from his wife is the worst possible thing he could have done. First, he has put his daughter in an impossible situation, causing harm that may require future therapy to undo. Marjorie is now in a double bind–by doing what she believes is best for one of her parents, she is being disloyal to the other. Whichever choice she makes, she will be hurting one of her parents. In addition, Michael has undermined his ability to be an effective parent to Marjorie, who is now in a position to pressure him to get preferential treatment compared to her siblings. Depending on her personality, Marjorie may feel a loss of respect for her mother and a sense of superiority to her, since she is now in possession of information that her mother doesn't have. Second, when Martha eventually learns, as she is likely to, of both the cybersex behavior and of the cover-up effort involving daughter Marjorie, she is likely to be so angry that reconciliation may be impossible.

In addition to problems involving children and secrets, another difficult scenario is the initially incomplete disclosure that results in sequential or staggered revelations. This situation, usually due to an effort to evade the consequences of one's behaviors, was discussed in detail in chapter 3. Our recommendation is to avoid this problem by initially divulging the outline of all the secrets, while avoiding specific details. Do not omit a significant part of the acting out; it will only make things worse in the long run. In this chapter we will discuss good and bad ways of handling the situations listed below. These include:

- When a slip or relapse has occurred, so that additional disclosure is necessary

- When one member of a couple has acquired a sexually transmitted disease/infection or health problem due to addict's sharing dirty needles

- When one partner has already decided to leave

- When long-ago secrets have not been revealed; timing of disclosure

- When the secret involves a friend, neighbor, or colleague.

- When the parent is not the biological parent

- When you are gay or lesbian

If you have not already made a list of other issues you need to address through disclosure, now is a good time to do so. Have you had a slip or relapse that you have not revealed? Anything else? Identify what will be the hardest part of these disclosures for you.

How Can I Possibly Tell Him/Her About My Relapse?

Sometimes staggered or sequential disclosures occur, not because the addict is deliberately hiding some information or has forgotten some events, but rather because a slip or relapse has occurred and there are now new secrets to uncover, new lies to reveal.

As mentioned in Chapter 5, we recommend that at the time of the first disclosure the partner determine how much information she wants to hear. After the initial revelations are worked through, the couple needs to decide what information the partner wants on an ongoing basis. Some partners want to know when someone has a slip and what the addict is doing to get his recovery back in line. Others want the addict to take that information to his or her sponsor or therapist, but do want to know if the addict has relapsed in ways that will harm the partner.

Unfortunately, the partner is often so in shock or angry and hurt that it takes a while to get clear about what to share. Revisiting what the partner wants to be told several times during first couple of years of recovery is important.

It is not easy to be honest in this situation. Perhaps your partner has told you, "If you ever use again, you're history." Or perhaps you and your partner have spent months rebuilding trust, and you believe that learning about your slip or relapse will set your partner's level of trust back to zero. Perhaps you feel so much shame at your "failure" that you cannot bring yourself to confess what happened.

Understand that this is a common experience. In our most recent research on disclosure of relapse (Corley, Schneider & Hook, 2012), we found that over 75% of the addicts reported they had experienced multiple relapses. When relapse happens, a decision about a new disclosure must be made. Below are the reactions of several spouses to hearing about a partner's relapse:

A woman who decided to stay with her husband after he had another affair wrote,

> I was very upset. He had had such great sobriety. I thought we had beaten his addiction and that it was 'history.' I shared about the effects of the relapse on me at my COSA meetings and had other people to talk to. I knew the behavior was about him, not me, but still I was really disappointed. We had been separated for 2 years while he was acting out, but this time I didn't even consider another separation. We wouldn't put our son through that again. As I saw it, we could each continue working on our individual recovery, or we could divorce if we felt there was nothing to work on.

Another woman reported she has learned a lot from her husband's relapses:

When my husband had his first relapse just after his first birthday in the program, I was totally shocked; he was one of the stars of the program. I was angry, hurt, and scared. When three months later there was another relapse, I wasn't very shocked, and experienced much less anger. The second time I didn't process as much anger with him – instead I processed with COSA and Al-Anon people and in my journal. I have grown a tremendous amount as a result of the two relapses. I have moved from dependence on him to dependence on myself and on being a 'big' person.

Yet another woman is considering divorce after learning of several relapses:

When I finally was told the truth about his relapse I chose to accept that as an addict, he fell off the wagon, just like taking one more drink or drug. That allowed me to be at peace and accepting of him. After two years and two more relapses, I realize that this is a process and that nothing is black or white. I am, though, at a point in my life where my tolerance for "gray" has worn as thin as it can. I am considering divorce.

In each of the cases above, the spouse was knowledgeable about the disease of addiction and aware that relapse is always a possibility. Each spouse had had experience with a Twelve Step program for information and support. Each one was able to separate the addict's behavior from herself and not "take it personally," and could rationally consider her choices rather than respond out of neediness and fear of being alone. In the last case, because the relapses were continuing, the wife was considering an end to the marriage.

The partner's response might have been very different if she were not herself in recovery and if she did not understand the nature of addictive disorders and the need to detach from the behaviors. In such a situation, her fear might be greater and her tolerance for a less-than-perfect recovery greater. She would most likely believe that the addict's problem had been "cured" and would be less likely to accept the relapsing nature of the disorder.

A relapse involving another person is likely to be more threatening to the partner and to be considered a more serious betrayal than is behavior involving only the addict. For example, if a sex addict masturbated or accessed pornography on the Internet instead of using a prostitute, the disclosure would be less threatening to a partner. Or if an alcoholic left the bar after one drink rather than getting drunk and driving drunk with his children in the car, the partner would be more able to view the relapse as less serious.

In our research on relapse we found it makes a significant difference in how your partner views you and the relationship if *you* reveal the slip or relapse before your partner discovers it. In fact, in those couples where the addict disclosed, they reported significantly more satisfaction with the relationship, were emotionally closer, had a more satisfying sexual relationship and reported higher levels of trust than did the couples in which the partner discovered the relapse. That is why we recommend, that as hard as it is to face a serious slip or relapse, it is better to talk about what to do if (or when) it happens.

When you are considering how and when to divulge a slip or relapse to your partner, there are several factors to consider. Below are listed some questions that will prepare you to make a subsequent disclosure.

1) List the changes you have made in response to the slip or relapse (For example, increasing your Twelve-Step involvement, reconnecting with or getting a new sponsor, making your environment safer, beginning or resuming therapy, etc.) You are likely to have a more positive and understanding reaction to your disclosure if you are taking steps to learn from the relapse and prevent it from happening again. If you have made *no* changes, then identify the changes you need to make and start making those immediately.

2) Write out the exact nature of the slip. You may even want to do what is called a "relapse autopsy." This is where you not only describe the exactly what happened, but you also identify everything that contributed to the "death" of your recovery efforts. What were the triggers that occurred? Did you find yourself in such an emotional situation in a high-risk environment that it "just happened" before you were even aware that you were acting out? Did you make seemingly unimportant decisions that contributed to getting in that wrong environment? For example, you decide to go on the Internet on your iPad just to find out what movies are showing to surprise your wife by inviting her to the movies this weekend (when you know that using the Internet when

alone is dangerous for you). Did the acting out put you (and therefore your spouse) at risk of a sexually transmitted disease? If so, an early disclosure is more urgent – set up a time for that now. Additionally, since you are taking that kind of risk for your health as well as your spouse, perhaps intensifying therapy or going to residential treatment is the next step to really getting a handle on the problem. If you are continuing to put your partner and yourself in harm's way with the knowledge you have about addiction and recovery, the problem needs to be addressed more seriously.

3) Is your spouse or partner involved in his or her own recovery program and/or in counseling? A partner who is not working on herself is likely to be more frightened of a slip or relapse, more likely to continue perceiving herself as a victim, and less likely to be empathetic to the addict's struggles. Sometimes when the partner has not been in a recovery program herself, she remains caught in her anger and resentment. This may be a partner who has an anxious attachment style, fears intimacy and can use the addict's behavior as a way to obtain distance and derive energy from the drama. This partner does not do well when hearing about slips, much less relapses. The information becomes fuel for the fire of anger. In such a case, it would be helpful to come clean within a therapy session.

4) Do you and your partner have a supportive environment in which to carry out the disclosure? The ideal setting is in a therapy session, after you have had a chance to discuss the relapse with the therapist. Twelve-Step sponsors, or another couple in recovery, are other possible resources.

5) Is a slip (a minor relapse), of a sufficiently serious nature as to (a) interfere with your maintaining a "program of rigorous honesty" in your recovery, or (b) likely to affect your primary relationship more adversely if it is revealed than if it is not? Divulging all slips is not always in the best interest of the relationship. For example, if you fantasized about another woman while making love with your wife last night, will it really benefit your marriage to reveal this? Or let's say you accepted a beer from a friend at the baseball game last night. If this event was a break in your addiction recovery plan, it might be more appropriate to discuss this with a sponsor or therapist rather than your wife. You and your partner should determine what must be told versus

what is better revealed to another support system and if your partner wants to know the steps you are taking to make changes in thoughts and actions.

I've Exposed Her/Him to a Health Risk. What Now?

Most of the time the addict has some time to consider exactly when and how to reveal painful information to the partner. However, in certain cases there is pressure to tell immediately. One such situation was discussed above – if your child, your boss, or the law has information that you believe they will soon reveal to your partner. The consensus among partners is that it is far better for them to hear the information from you than from other people.

Another situation requiring urgent action is when you have caught or possibly been infected with a virus or other infection as a result of unprotected sexual interactions or sharing needles. (Any activity with another person that involves sharing even the smallest quantity of bodily fluid can be the entrance route of a virus or other infection.) Not all infections show symptoms immediately, so thinking you can wait for the results of medical tests puts you and your partner at risk. Your partner may need to visit a doctor for evaluation and possible treatment. At the very least, you will need to begin using condoms or to abstain from sex or other activities with your partner that might spread the infection. In both cases, your partner will need an explanation and the sooner the better. We know of several partners who chose to leave the marriage because they felt that the biggest betrayal they'd experienced was that their mate continued to expose them to health risks. One of them told us,

> He had shared needles and had unprotected sex with other men, and then he'd have sex with me. We have two young children. He put his own pleasure above my life and potentially, that of our children! He was willing to expose me to a fatal disease. When I finally found out, all I wanted to do was put as much distance as possible between us. We are now divorced. Thank heavens I didn't catch anything from him.

Painful and risky though it may be to admit to your partner that she or he is at risk for an STD or other health problem, it shows caring, and your partner will eventually recognize this. On the flip side, the message a partner gets when the addict repeatedly exposes her to HIV, hepatitis, chlamydia and other diseases is that he just doesn't care. Postponing this disclosure makes it far more likely that the eventual outcome will be the end of the relationship.

When Long-Ago Secrets Have Not Been Revealed

Jay had been in recovery from his sex addiction for two years when he and Monica had dinner out with friends one evening. In a conversation about "the old days," Jay recalled how three years earlier, he and Monica had had a fight and she backed out of accompanying him out of town on a business trip. Upset with her, he'd phoned a stripper to visit him in his hotel room. Monica clearly remembered what Jay had told her at the time to explain the charge on his credit card, and she now chimed into the conversation: "and when he actually saw the stripper, she was so unattractive that Jay paid her and sent her away." Jay looked at her as though she must be insane.

"I would never have done that!" He readily admitted that they'd had sex. Monica was livid. Once they were alone in the parking lot, she angrily confronted him.

"You lied to me! You told me you'd sent her away! How could you have done this? How can I ever trust you?"

Jay sighed and looked at her wearily, "Monica, before I got into recovery I told you so many lies that I no longer remember exactly what I said. Lying was so much a part of my life back then that I lied even when I didn't have to. I'm sorry about this particular lie, but I'm sure that there will be other occasions when you will realize I lied in the past. All I can say is I haven't lied to you once since I got into recovery two years ago, and I intend to continue being honest with you. That's the best I can say."

Monica realized that what he said made sense, and that she would have to accept the possibility of other lies without getting upset all over again. For two years Jay had given her no reason to doubt his word. She would have to draw a line between the "bad old days" and the time in recovery, and judge them differently. She would have to forgive the past, meaning to be able to hear about it without getting upset all over again. Part of the task of doing this turned out to be a period of grieving the loss of the past as she had previously perceived it. Instead, she had to accept that her life with Jay had been a web of lies and deceptions, not the great marriage she thought she had.

When a Parent is Not the Biological Parent

Another situation involves a long-ago secret kept from a child. One such dilemma was described in a 2011 column in the New York Times column called "The Ethicist." A man wrote,

> *"I didn't find out for years, but I fathered a child with a woman who was, and still is, married to another man. The girl does not know any of this. Neither does the husband. At the mother's request, I have had nothing to do with the girl. . . Does the girl have a right to know her true parentage upon reaching adulthood? Sooner? Over the objection of the mother? Only when the husband dies? Who can make these decisions and when?"*

The columnist's reply was that such information could have devastating consequences for the entire family – or the outcome could be very good, explaining to the girl some clues she may have long perceived. The mother is the person in the best position to evaluate the best option, and her judgment should not be overruled. "If you feel strongly that the girl should know, talk to her mother and try to reach a consensus – a consensus that would eventually, if painfully, have to include the woman's husband."

Recent research on adopted children and those born as a result of donated sperm and/or eggs has shown that such children very often want information about their biological parents or egg or sperm donor. They are very curious about where they came from. Professional organizations such as the American Society for Reproductive Medicine, and adoption agencies now recommend disclosing to children, most commonly before puberty. Some European countries no longer permit anonymous gamete donations. But when the child's conception involved secrecy and betrayal on the part of one parent, then there are obviously complex issues to be resolved around making this decision.

When the Secret Involves a Neighbor or Friend

Susan lives in a subdivision consisting of many homes with the same floor plan. One day she notices that her next-door neighbor Ike is peeping into the bedroom window of another neighbor across the street. She thinks this is odd, but soon forgets about it. A few days later she again sees Ike standing outside the neighbor's bedroom window. Should Susan confront Ike? Tell Ike's wife? Call the police? Tell the neighbor who'd been spied on?

Again, there are no clear-cut answers. Susan's decision is likely to be influenced by her relationship with the people involved. She may decide to have no direct contact with the neighbors but rather only to call the police. After all, it's not her responsibility to tell the wife. The wife might not appreciate another woman calling her and telling her that her husband is a voyeur. She might become angry and threatening, and might blame the messenger. The police might interview the man, which would certainly catch his attention and make it more likely he will get help. Even if the police don't do anything, they will have a record of the incident in case they are notified that he was caught in another voyeuristic act.

Susan might decide to tell the police, and also to tell the voyeur, advising him to tell his wife before the police do. Susan might instead notify the wife, believing that she is the one who has the most leverage and is most likely to be able to pressure him into treatment. Also, the wife might want to be told – this might not be the first time, and she may be already aware of the behavior or suspects it. (Of course, the wife may well be aware of the voyeur's activities and has had no luck in getting him to get help). Moreover, if the police are involved, and the man arrested, it could well have adverse consequences for the wife and children, so better to begin by telling the wife. Whether or not to speak to the man's wife would depend on the relationship between the two women. If they were friends, the wife would more likely want Susan to alert her to the situation if she were not already aware of it. Finally, Susan might decide to notify the neighbor who had been spied on, on the grounds that the neighbor had been the victim and needs to know so she can decide whether to notify the police as well as how to protect herself in the future.

Once again, there is often no one right answer. No wonder it is difficult for the average person to decide what to disclose, how much, to whom, and when!

Addressing Something You Did Years Ago

If you knew you were an addict before you got involved with your partner, but you failed to inform her, then you need to make amends for not fully informing her of your past. In our research on disclosure of sexual addiction, we asked if partners knew or addicts told about the addiction prior to marriage or commitment to their partner. The majority said no or very little was disclosed. (We would also add that in relationships in which the addict told the partner about his/her addiction prior to commitment, addicts and partners reported more satisfaction in their relationships than those who did not tell prior to commitment.)

While we recommend that if a relationship is serious enough to go beyond the third date or if one decides to engage in sexual intercourse, then information that one is an addict (in recovery if that is accurate) should be shared. Also let the person know that with addiction comes responsibilities for recovery (and then you can outline some of those such as going to Twelve-Step meetings, drug screens, limitations of use of Internet, etc.)

Another question is how much to reveal about long-ago behavior, especially behavior that happened before your current relationship. This is a time to keep information general, such as "I was involved in casual, but addictive sexual encounters early in my addiction. I did not realize I was a sex addict." Or "I experimented with all sorts of drugs when I was young, but never used IV drugs." If your partner wants more information, it is useful to understand why it is important to your partner to know this. Sometimes it makes perfect sense to answer more questions; other times it may seem that it is adding to your partner's distress. It can be helpful to utilize a therapist to guide you and your partner through this.

A different situation is when you have engaged in behaviors that have the potential to be harmful to another person. A man in his early forties recalled that when he was just twenty-one he had fondled his thirteen-year-old cousin in her sleep. He was not sure if she had actually been asleep or was just faking sleep. He had not seen her for several years but they were close when she was in her teens. He did not want to cause her distress with a disclosure but also wanted to be honest with her about behavior he knew was wrong.

This man had victimized his cousin, crossing sexual boundaries with a minor. But even if she had been an adult, engaging in a sexual behavior without consent is victimizing. The victim should have a say in whether she wants more information and certainly should receive amends. He could say something like, "Since I am older and now in recovery from sexual addiction, I realize I did some things with you when you were young that were not right and I want to make amends. Since it was a long time ago, I do not want to make things worse with details but know that you have a right to know what I did. I hope you will accept my amends. You may want to think about it more and might have questions. If you do, I am willing to answer any questions you might have." There is nothing worse for a victim to have a sense that something happened, but then to not really know. Verification of a "feeling" or "sense" can be helpful for a victim to heal. Our research has consistently shown that people who are betrayed want the disclosure; they would rather know and be able to make decisions based on truth.

However, when a minor was involved, as is the case with molesting a thirteen-year old, legal consequences must be considered. First, in some states there is no statute of limitations for child abuse; in these states the therapist is obligated to report the client to authorities, no matter how many years have elapsed. The client may end up being arrested and imprisoned. It is also highly desirable to assess the offender's motivation – for example, is it to help the survivor's healing, or is it to relieve his own guilt? The results of the disclosure are unpredictable: If the woman feels traumatized she may take legal action.

A Friend's Spouse is Having an Affair, Using Drugs, or Gambling Compulsively

A closely related and more common ethical dilemma is what to do if you learn that the spouse of your close friend is having an affair or any other addictive behavior. Do you tell your close friend? The late Dr. Shirley Glass, author of *NOT Just Friends*, a psychologist specializing in infidelity, related that she usually advises confronting the offending person first and advises the person to tell the partner; if not, then you will do it. The reason is that otherwise the friendship is ruined because it is too uncomfortable to be carrying those kinds of secrets. In her experience, Dr. Glass told us, "When the betrayed partner later found out that other people knew, they were very hurt and angry. In many cases, the relationships were permanently severed because they focused their feelings of betrayal on the colluder who could be a potential informant." Interestingly, in Dr. Glass's experience, when someone does eventually tell the betrayed partner about the affair, it is most commonly the affair partner, who presumably wanted to drive a further wedge between her lover and his spouse. "It usually backfired because the crisis it evoked was a catalyst to stop the affair and rebuild the marriage."

We have known sex addicted women involved in affairs with married men who tell the wife as an external intervention for themselves. The sex addicted women knew that telling the wife would likely end the affair when the addict was not able to.

The stories in this chapter represent some real-life situations. The correct approach is not always clear; gray areas abound. As we have seen, determining the best course involves, above all, communication. If you are uncertain about whether to disclose or keep a secret, about whether telling will help or hurt your partner, your recovery, and/or your relationship, consult others. Talk with a sponsor, a counselor, or a friend. Sometimes the uncertainty remains. You may need to follow your heart and take the risk of opening your heart to your partner, even if the outcome is uncertain.

When You are Gay or Lesbian and Coming Out to Your Partner

Addicted men and women can have sexual encounters with same-sex partners for a variety of reasons. A disclosure about that behavior is the same as outlined in Chapter 5. This section is about being gay or lesbian and coming out to your straight partner.

While society has become more accepting of homosexuality and same-sex marriage/unions, for many it is still a difficult process to accept one's own sexual identity and then to go public about it. It is fairly common for people who are avoiding dealing with their gay or lesbian identity to medicate their emotional distress with a variety of addictive behaviors, especially for those who were raised in an era in which being gay or lesbian was less accepted.

Because of the stigma that has been associated with homosexuality, it is logical that gays and lesbians would decide that marrying a straight partner would be the answer. Some hope that this straight marriage will "cure" their attraction and desire to be with a same-gender partner. Others just want a cover and believe they can lead a "secret life" without hurting anyone. Many fall in love with their straight partners, have children, and live the life that they believe is expected of them – for a while, but then the emotional distress and desire for a same-sex partner comes back and for most, over time gets worse.

If you have now figured out that you have not been fair to or honest with yourself, your spouse, or others important to you by living this secret life and have decided to "come out", preparing to disclose is the same as any other disclosure but there is a difference. Be clear – you are not saying you were wrong to be gay/lesbian. You are saying that you are sorry to have lied (and for other behaviors that might have put your partner at risk for their physical and emotional health or their finances.)

It is helpful to determine in what stage of coming out you are so that that information can be shared with your partner. You may be ambivalent about whether you want to stay in this marriage, but also want to engage in homo-social activities that honor your gay or lesbian identity. Examples are socializing with gay/lesbian friends, getting involved in gay/lesbian social events, going to GLBT events, and attending religious services at institutions that cater to GLBT members, activities that honor your gay or lesbian identify while still living in your current marriage. Perhaps you have already decided that you feel no love or friendship with your partner and that you don't want to stay in this heterosexual marriage. You may have children and want to explore staying married but also living an open or private gay lifestyle. All these factors play a role.

Many straight partners have some suspicion that their mate is gay or have same- sex attraction; others don't know. No matter what is known, often partners react to the disclosure with shock, confusion, fear, anger, and sadness. We have never witnessed a disclosure that is not painful, but hearing you have been living a lie is hard for anyone.

At the point of disclosure it is usually too early for your partner to know if she or he wants to stay married. Some partners feel a sense of relief because there have been sexual problems in the relationship and now they know why; others want to stay in the marriage and to continue to enjoy the emotional connection, but no longer want to be sexual. Some just don't understand what happened, end up blaming themselves, and want to try some other kind of therapy to save the marriage. Some are bitter and feel betrayed but insist on staying married out of confusion, spite, fear of being alone, or for financial or health reasons. While on one level you may be feeling positive about the work you have done to accept your orientation and hopeful about your future, at disclosure this is almost always a painful time for everyone.

All of this is why planning this event with your therapist is a good idea. And careful planning for support for your partner is a must. Amity Pierce Buxton (1994) reports that many partners become depressed and isolated, are too embarrassed to tell friends or family members, and have little knowledge of how to get support. So planning well for your partner is very important. An excellent website for partners is the Straight Spouse Network (www.ssnetwk.org). It is loaded with resources including answers to many questions partners have and support group websites in many communities.

Expect her or him to grive for a period of time. You may have already spent months or even years working through your own identity issues and are only now ready to come out to your partner, but this is new to him or her. Despite your previous work, when you experience your partner's grief, you will grieve as well. Be patient, feel your feelings, and support your partner in feeling her or his. It gets better.

When You or Your Spouse Really Wants to Leave

After years of struggling in his troubled marriage, 50-year old Arthur was ready to call it quits with Angie. He progressively distanced himself emotionally, and finally got involved in an affair with a younger woman he'd met at the company where he was doing some consulting work.

Perhaps on some level Arthur wanted Angie to find out; perhaps he was hoping that if she caught him, Angie would demand a divorce, so that he wouldn't have to take the initiative himself. At any rate, he left enough clues around that it didn't take Angie long to figure out what was happening.

Her response, however, was not what he'd been expecting. Instead of announcing the end of the marriage, Angie took all the blame on herself and insisted on going to counseling to try to save the relationship. Not wanting to hurt her even more, Arthur couldn't face telling Angie directly that he wanted to leave, so he reluctantly assented to joint counseling.

In preliminary individual sessions, the counselor learned that Arthur had emotionally left the marriage years earlier. He explained to Arthur that couple counseling is likely to be effective only if both partners have the same goal. In Arthur's case, he was only prolonging and postponing the pain that Angie would inevitably feel at learning the truth. The counselor persuaded Arthur to reveal to Angie in a joint session that, for him, the marriage was irretrievably broken.

Acknowledging a painful secret can be made less painful for the partner if it is accompanied by a declaration of a commitment to the relationship. If you and your partner have a long history together, many memories of good times, and perhaps children, it may be very difficult to admit that the marriage has ended for you, especially if you believe that this will be devastating for your partner.

As we will see in Chapter 9, however, for those who whose marriage ends, there is life after divorce, even for the one who still feels committed to the marriage. Although at first, life without you may indeed seem to be hardly worth living, soon enough your former partner will reclaim herself or himself and realize that life has much to offer. People who are in a recovery program can call on the support of their Twelve-Step program, program friends, counselor, and the tools of the program and can indeed become contented and fulfilled. While we do caution against acting too quickly about the future of a marriage after a disclosure, if your marriage has been over for some time, tell your partner and let him/her begin to heal from the loss.

References

Buxton, Amity Pierce, *Other Side of the Closet: The Coming Out Crisis for Straight Spouses.* New York: Wiley (1994).

Corley, M. Deborah, Scheider, Jennifer P. and Hook, Joshua. Partners' decision-making after disclosure of sexual addiction relapse *Sexual Addiction & Compulsivity,* 2012, in press.

Chapter Eight
Special Issues

Disclosing to your partner and children is extremely difficult for everyone involved. The addict who comes clean usually experiences an immediate sense of relief. The experiences for the partner and children, however, are varied. Matters are further complicated when one has to decide what to say at work, with family members and friends, or within your faith community.

Family Members

Depending on your relationship with your parents, siblings, and other extended family members, most addicts and partners want family members to have some information. If you are estranged from family members, then you may decide to keep private the information about the addiction. However, if family members provide emotional support for you, it is important that they have general knowledge of what is going on in your life. There may be other members of your family who are dealing with similar problems or have dealt with them and can be of help to you. Some addicts can identify generations of other family members who have struggled with addictions:

> *I come from a family of drinkers, lots of depression, and abuse of prescription drugs. My great grandfather made "white lightning" and sold it during the Depression. He was known to be able to drink the stuff and it not affect him. My own father was depressed and drank heavily, which did not help matters. Then he crushed his hand in an accident at work. He was on pain medication and had disability. The longer he could show he was in pain, the longer he got to stay on disability. Before long, he was addicted to the pills—which he drank alcohol with. It is a wonder it did not kill him. Then I come along and do about the same thing—just without the alcohol. I am recovering from addiction to prescription drugs (Xanax and*

Vicodin). Now my son is in treatment for addiction to marijuana and alcohol. It's scary. I wonder if it will ever end.

Being exposed to addictive behavior happens in a variety of ways:

I found my Dad's pornography collection when I was 8. He was a drinker and I was pretty sure he had sex with other women because I saw him once with a woman, not my mother, downtown. My Mom would accuse him and they'd yell and he'd be out the door. It wasn't long before I was using those images from that porn, masturbating to shut out my whole lousy life—their fights, being smaller than other guys my age, never measuring up. I am sure pornography and masturbation were my introduction to sex addiction. It worked like magic—felt so good, let me fantasize that I was "somebody". It took me away from my problems but I didn't stop there. I used the pornography to make friends with other guys. It wasn't long before I was introduced to sex by an older neighborhood boy. When I went to treatment and talked to my Dad, he admitted that he had problems with affairs and pornography too. He said his grandfather was known as a ladies' man—I never knew him but wonder if he was a sex addict, too.

The same principles apply for telling close family members as do for telling your partner. Provide only general information that may be educational as well, but leave out the details. It is also helpful at this juncture to apologize for any ways your behavior may have hurt them. You and your partner need to decide what you will reveal and what you want to keep private between the two of you. The addict should acknowledge his behavior and addiction, the partner her behavior and addictions, if applicable.

In the box is a sample letter of what might be said to parents who are supportive and with whom the addict and partner feel close:

Dad and Mom:
    I want to thank you for meeting me. What I have to say is very important and it is important to me that you are willing to do this. The purpose of this meeting is not to blame anyone for anything—what I have done is my responsibility alone. My purpose is to let you know what has been going on with me and Susan and what I plan to do about it.

You may not know that Susan and I have been having problems. We are pretty good at keeping secrets. I have been very good at keeping secrets, not only from Susan, but from everyone.

For many years I have been using sex like a drug—like a drug addict would, to make me feel better when I feel anxious, or depressed, sad, or mad. Sometimes I use it when I feel good because I don't know how to deal with feeling good either. The point is, I don't know how to handle how I feel and I learned early in life that one way to do it is through a sexual release. Some people call this sex addiction, so I now call myself a sex addict.

I don't want to tell you all the details of what I do because that is something I deal with in therapy and with Susan. I am also in a Twelve-Step program much like Alcoholics Anonymous and it is helping me learn how to handle my feelings. In therapy I am learning more how to have confidence in myself, and Susan and I are working on how to be healthy together.

I want to say again, I am not blaming you or anyone for how I am. Lots of people hear that someone becomes a sex addict because of something that happened in their childhood. I have come to believe that lots of things from my childhood influenced how I saw the world and responded to it, but now I am an adult and can make adult choices in responsible ways. I am grateful to you for all you have done for me. I know you did the best you could to raise me well.

There are lots of books you can read to find out more about sex addiction. I can recommend a few and I am willing to answer some questions. The only questions I won't respond to are those that Susan and I want to keep between us.

I need your support and love now. I am sorry for the hardship this has caused everyone involved and for the worry I have caused you. I am better and have great hope for the future.

I love you.

Your son, Al.

Then ask them—Do you have any questions or anything you want to say now?

Many addicts and partners have been the victims of sexual trauma within their families of origin, and are in a delicate position with regard to disclosing. However, disclosure can provide freedom from shame and help a survivor move forward in his/her recovery.

If a part of your history is that you are a survivor of sexual trauma, you may want to talk with your therapist about how to handle resolution of those issues as part of the disclosure process. If those issues have been addressed in your family of origin and you feel safe within that family system, telling is appropriate. Ending the family secrets is an important step to stopping the multigenerational transmission of these traits.

Often survivors are tempted to blame parents for the sexual abuse the survivor endured. It is important to obtain therapy for childhood sexual trauma. Remember, *the therapy for holding the victimizer accountable is different from disclosure. Disclosure is important in order for you to be accountable for your behavior.* It is appropriate, nonetheless, for survivors to include, as part of their disclosure, the boundaries they need to make public. An example is shown in the next box:

Dad:

    The purpose of this letter and our meeting is for me to explain what I have been doing that is very unhealthy for me. I also want to talk about what I have learned about myself in therapy, what I am doing to help myself, and what I would like you to do to help me with this.

    I learned early in my life that I could make men do things for me by having sex with them. Having sex with men made me feel powerful and that I had control over them. This may be related to the sexual interactions between you and me, but I am not blaming you for my behavior. I am responsible for what I have done and the choices I have made. I started using sex like a drug and my life got out of control because I took more and more chances to feel powerful and to cover how bad I felt about myself inside. I am a sex and love addict. I've hurt my kids, my husband, the people who are important to me in my life, and mostly, I have hurt myself.

    But I am doing better now. I am going to Twelve-Step meetings, therapy, and even though Bob and I are getting divorced, I am getting along better with him, too. I am learning to be a better mom.

    To help me with my recovery, I have a couple of requests. First, when we are together, I need to have more space. I get anxious when you want to put your arms around me all the time. I also get uncomfortable when you talk about your girlfriends and about having sex with them. I'd like us to focus on talking about the kids, work, the weather, movies, or things like that. If you have some problem with me, then it is okay to tell me about it and I will do the same with you. Then we both can make decisions like adults about what to do next. In the past, I've made matters worse when we disagreed by yelling at you and then at my kids. For now, I'd like no touching until we are about to leave, then a brief hug is okay.

I appreciate that you have listened and that you came to talk to me today. Do you have any questions?

Setting boundaries to help you maintain your recovery is important. This is an appropriate time for the survivor to do it.

A New Love Relationship

When an addict begins a new relationship, many people are not clear when or if to tell the new person in their life about their addiction. All addicts are at risk for relapse, no matter how long you have been sober. Informing a potential mate is important. But when to tell is determined by the type of addiction, any legal issues involved, and the seriousness of the relationship.

Many addicts say that they are not going to divulge their past until they are sure this person is "the one." Unfortunately this can backfire because a potential mate will take it as a lack of trust and, in some instances, a form of dishonesty that you did not open up before the relationship became serious.

Certainly, it is not wise to tell anyone new in your life all your story, but after a few dates, beginning to "test the waters" about how someone will respond to the knowledge that you attend Twelve-Step meetings or that you go to a group to work on learning better ways of coping can open the door for further discussions.

Most people are pretty accepting of drug addiction or gambling and food issues; people are less likely to respond positively and more likely to jump to conclusions when it comes to sex addiction. Preparation of a disclosure letter is a good idea, including information about addiction in general. As indicated above, sharing general information about your addiction first is safest. If you are still in the early stages of recovery (first couple of years), a new love relationship is probably premature and it's best to slow down. New relationships cause people to feel more energy and excitement, but that energy is due to the chemicals your brain makes. Realistically, these relationships take a great deal of energy and time—sometimes compromising your recovery.

If you are in new relationship and believe you are ready to become more serious, a conversation about the desire to move to the next level is a good way to start. State that one of your values is that people in intimate friendships should have enough trust in each other to tell each other the truth and not keep secrets. Indicate that the relationship has grown to a degree that you believe it is time to disclose information that for the most part is private in your life.. Then give general information about your addiction and the type of acting out that you do. This is easier if you are a drug addict or some other behavioral addict; Accept that sexual information of any kind just makes people nervous. .

Latoya was a gambling addict. Although she had abused alcohol and had smoked cigarettes for years, gambling was her main route to escape her feelings of inadequacy and her fear of her first husband's temper. She gambled in isolation and secrecy. Her first marriage had ended in divorce. It took her seven years to get her gambling under control and her finances back in order. Dating was long in coming and she was very careful while early in recovery to go to social events with a group of friends. . Eventually she met a man close to her age, Washington, who was also divorced and who had two children. Initially she accepted invitations to accompany Washington to church and then other activities which included his children. After Washington started to ask her to dinner and the movies without the children, Latoya was convinced that Washington was getting as serious as she felt. This is what she shared with him about her addiction:

> *Washington, I am so fond of you and your children. You have done such a wonderful job of raising them. I feel like our relationship is getting pretty serious and like I owe you much. Part of what I owe you is the truth about me. If we are going to have some type of commitment to each other in the future, I think you deserve to know this about me.*
>
> *I am a gambling addict. That is why I go to meetings at the church on Wednesday and Saturdays—I go to meetings for my addiction then. I also used to drink heavily when I gambled, and I smoked. That is why I don't drink now and was attracted to you because you don't smoke. My first marriage was rough and I used gambling to escape my feelings. I was not able to face my fear of my husband*

and in the end I only made him angrier because I forced us into such debt. Even after we divorced, when I had basically nothing, I stole money from him and continued to write checks on our old account. I was just lucky I did not get into trouble legally. I had to file bankruptcy and am just now beginning to get my credit reestablished.

I have seven years of solid recovery with no relapses, but I know as an addict I will never be totally free of this disease. That is why I still go to meetings after all these years—they help me stay grounded, help others, and remind me of where I have been. I hope this doesn't change things between us—you mean the world to me and I would hate for our friendship to end.

This disclosure had a happy ending. Washington appreciated Latoya's honesty and was encouraged by her long-term recovery. Latoya and Washington were married about a year later. Washington supports Latoya in her efforts to sponsor other addicts as well as tell her story in the church where they attend services.

George had a more difficult task with Evelyn. George had been an alcohol and sex addict for as long as he could remember. He stopped drinking many years before but despite three attempts at sex addiction treatment, he struggled for almost 15 years of regular relapses. During this process he had met a wonderful woman from his church. Both devout Catholics, they discovered they loved many of the same things. Because they were Catholic, they had taken a vow of celibacy but spoke often of marriage. Determined not to lose Evelyn, George gave her a beautiful two-carat diamond engagement ring when he asked her to marry him. Evelyn was very excited and wanted to marry soon, but George kept finding ways to postpone the ceremony because he had not been able to go more than five weeks without a relapse on Internet pornography and masturbation or engaging in anonymous sex with masseurs. Finally, through the support of individual therapy, his men's group, and medication for his depression and intrusive thinking, he experienced several months of sobriety. He agreed to set a date for marriage but was determined not to reveal his sex addiction to Evelyn.

It was in his men's group that he became convinced that he had to tell Evelyn. He had had sex with others while engaged to her. Not only that, but he'd had unsafe sex while acting out. All seven men in his group agreed that continued secret-keeping would not help his recovery nor be fair to Evelyn. One of his peers in group commented, "If you cared as much for Evelyn as you have been saying for over a year now, I can't imagine how you could demonstrate that more than by giving her a chance to choose you as you are—addict and all." He knew then that it was the right thing to do and the only way he could remain sober. Keeping secrets was against everything he wanted in this marriage. With so much at risk, this is what he wrote in a disclosure letter to her:

Evelyn,

You have been a great sunshine in my life, a great gift of joy, a wonderful companion, the woman I love, with whom I want to spend the rest of my life. There are some things you need to know about me about my life. Some of them happened a long time ago. Some happened in the recent past.

The decision about which I have the greatest regret is that when I was twelve and my sister was six, I molested her. It was a single episode that involved only masturbation, but it greatly influenced my relationship with her. I was so ashamed of what I had done that I wanted my sister to disappear, simply to cease existing. So just seeing her was a reminder of my own guilt and shame. This caused the great damage in my relationship with my sister and underlies my present difficulties with her.

You should also know that once, about eight years ago, I was arrested for indecent exposure. I was masturbating in a booth that showed pornographic videos when a police officer opened the door to the booth and saw me. I was convicted of the crime, but received deferred adjudication and was on probation for six months. Finally, you should know that I have had sex with men. I do not believe that I am a homosexual. My addiction has grown out of extensive child-hood sexual abuse by men and imprinting of that abuse has led me to be sexual with men.

I have been in recovery for my alcohol and sex addiction for over fifteen years. This has involved attending thousands of meetings, years of therapy, and three separate stays at treatment facilities. It cannot be said that my efforts have been half-hearted. But whereas I long ago left my drinking behind me, my recovery from sex addiction, unfortunately, has been more difficult. I have not been perfect in my attempts to remain celibate. It is this lack of perfection during the time that we've been dating that I want to talk to you about today.

While we have been dating, I have continued to have sexual activity beyond the activity between us. Most of this activity has been masturbation, often combined with using pornography on the Internet. My greatest single problem has been Internet pornography. Not all of my sexual activity, however, has been by myself. I have had sexual contact with men, mostly with masseurs who have masturbated me. On two occasions I have received oral sex from men. It was immediately after that in desperation I sought out my therapist and began therapy with her and joined her group. Most recently, on two occasions while we were dating, I had sex with women, once about 2 1/2 years ago with a woman whom I contacted on a phone chat-line and once about a year ago with the woman to whom I went for a massage.

I am willing and fully prepared to let you know anything you want to know about my past sexual behavior beyond what I have spoken of. After I finish reading this prepared statement, I will answer any questions that you have.

You certainly must be asking yourself: how can he have done these things, these things he knew what hurt me deeply, these things so contrary to his faith and mine? How could he have done these things if he in fact loved me? Please do not doubt for a moment the depth of my love for you. I hope you have seen that love in my behavior, in the ways that you have seen that I have changed myself while I have been dating you. No, it is not a lack of love for you that leads to my addiction. Nor is it a lack of faith. My faith is deep and my faith is wide. It is the core of my life and the compass of my daily actions.

I think you've come to understand that my sex addiction is a means to relieve tension, stress, fear, and all manner of pain. While I have been dating you, the single most powerful factor in keeping me in my addiction has been the pain of knowing that I was keeping secrets from you. Nothing has caused me so much fear—the fear that if you knew the truth of my life, you would leave me—a loss

I felt I could not bear. Other sex addicts in recovery have told me that once they were completely honest with their spouses and lovers they were able to build a sounder, deeper love based on complete honesty. I hope that will be true for us as well. Believe me when I tell you that my willingness to tell you the truth, the willingness to risk losing you, is the greatest manifestation of my love for you. Many of my friends have told me what a great help their supportive wives have been to them. Up to now my best friend has been in the dark about what is going on with me. That is no longer true.

My therapist will tell you that there are no guarantees, that my recovery can never be more than daily reprieve contingent on the maintenance of my spiritual condition. I hope that she will tell you that she thinks that I am a pretty good bet. Yes, surely a bet, but a good one

All my love, George

While George thought he needed to get everything on the table, there was so much history and detail it was overwhelming for Evelyn. Although she felt shocked, she was also deeply moved by George's disclosure and the abuse he had endured.

At first, she was very disturbed and angry about his acting out during their engagement. It took her several therapy sessions to clarify the impact this information had on her and the relationship. She reported being more upset by the secret keeping than anything else. With time she learned more about addiction and she began to have more compassion for George and how difficult the disease had been for him to manage. Evelyn was grateful that George valued her enough to tell her before they were married so she could make an informed choice. She said if he had waited until after the wedding, she would have had the marriage annulled immediately. Through more couples counseling and a great deal of discussion with their priest, this couple was able to move ahead with their marriage plans within a year of the disclosure.

When You Are Not Sure You Are Really In Love

When an addict is actively in addiction, sometimes he thinks he is in love with his partner but then when he gets sober he is no longer so certain. If this has happened to you, rather than just going along as if you are in love, it is better to speak about this ambiguity. Here is a nice example from a gay addict speaking to his partner about his feelings about love and what he proposes. This was part of his disclosure process.

I care deeply for you. I am learning how to feel love and love myself and others. I am working hard to honor my feelings and accurately identify them. I am not sure that what I feel for you is love or friendship or respect or some combination of them. I would like to stay together to clarify what my feelings are now that I am in a sober state and in recovery. I hope you will give me the opportunity to develop a relationship with you based on honest sharing, genuine caring and love.

Friends

Sometimes it is easier to open up to close friends than to family. Again, the disclosure needs to reflect the closeness of the friendship, and how the friend may have been hurt during periods of acting out. If the addict has a relationship with a friend of his partner, the addict may want to disclose to the friend. However, in most cases, the partner tells the friend what she feels comfortable telling and uses the friendship as a means of support for her. Some partners unload all the details of the addict's behavior to the friend, who then aligns with the partner and becomes protective toward the partner and angry with the addict.

Be clear with your friend the role you want him or her to play. Your friend should be there to listen, reflect, and then ask questions or remind you of what you have said you want to do to change. If you want your friend to fight the battle for you, you will not learn.

Besides disclosing, tell your friend how he or she can help you. Be specific. Sometimes it is unclear to friends whether you are seeking support for leaving or you just want to vent. Let them know that venting helps you, but that you are not ready to give up the relationship with your partner (unless you are) and that all you need is for them to acknowledge what awareness you have gained and validate how difficult it is for you. If you have been out-of-control in your addiction and your friend has been a victim of your behavior, apologize for that and encourage him or her to remind you if he or she again sees you engaging in that type of behavior.

Friends are critical to recovery. If you have been acting out with friends but wish to continue seeing them now that you are in recovery, then you must reveal your addiction and the need to not engage in those behaviors when you are together. Sometimes sharing with "using" friends includes telling them that you can't see them anymore. This is a loss that requires grieving. (In fact, it is part of grieving the loss of your addiction.) Use the disclosure as a means to set a boundary and even say goodbye to "using" friends. In Raphael's case, he had to tell Luke they could no longer be friends. This is what he said:

Luke, hey man, it's good to see you. I'm glad we had this chance to talk because I have something that is very important to me to share with you. I have really been evaluating my life and how I've been doing stuff that is hurting my wife, my kids—me. It is even affecting my work. I had some great fun with you, going to bars, talking—but the drug use and even smoking—well, it really isn't who I want to be. I am pretty sure I am a drug addict and for sure addicted to cigarettes. But no matter if I am or am not, I know I have to stop doing that stuff. So it means I have to stop hanging around with you. I want you to know that this is not about you—I am not judging you. You've been there for me, but I can't take the chance that you'd want to do those things and then maybe I would too, so I wanted to tell you face to face because you've been my friend. I won't be calling and hope that you won't call me—unless you are interested in going to a Twelve-Step meeting with me for drug addicts! Good luck man. I'll keep hoping the best for you. Bye now.

Think about the friends you must leave behind because association with them is too high risk for your recovery. You might write a basic disclosure and good-bye letter to practice before setting a boundary and acknowledging to friends you need to stop associating with them.

For friends who can provide support for you, disclosure is important so that they know what you are dealing with. If you have hurt them with your behavior or have been keeping secrets within the friendship or have lied, then it is appropriate to admit and apologize for that kind of behavior. The level of friendship should dictate how much you tell. Some friends can hear the details and be supportive. Others cannot. Your best bet is to start slowly with general information, what you are doing to care for yourself, and what they can do to help. If you are willing to answer questions, report so. It is important to identify those friends who can be supportive and talk with them about how they can help you with your recovery.

Disclosure After An Arrest

There are certain circumstances in which one is forced to decide how to handle situations when other people find out. This may be because an arrest is made and a sheriff or police officer comes to your home or place of work and arrests you. Sometimes notification of the arrest is printed in the newspaper. If the arrest seems newsworthy, the media may get involved. Each of these situations prompts worry and curiosity by family members, neighbors, and co-workers.

If you're arrested, telling the truth to your partner is important, but the usual order of business is to get an attorney. Of course, tell your attorney everything. You are protected by attorney-client privilege, so what you say cannot be repeated without your permission. This can pose a problem with a partner who is unsure what is going on. Let your attorney guide you in these instances about your legal risks—but your recovery remains a priority, so try to work with your attorney about what you need for your recovery. If you act out while out on bond or on probation your case may be pretty much a sunk ship!

When legal cases have not been settled, often you have to tell those who are important to you that you cannot speak about the case per the attorney's advice, but that you need their support. Look for ways people can help—respite care for the children, cooking a meal, providing a shoulder to cry on.

Sometimes enough information is already public that you are forced to say something. If your "case" has been publicized through the media, and they are approaching you, your family, or a neighbor, decide what you are going to say to the media with your partner and run it by your attorney. Frequently a "no comment" stance or "you can speak with my attorney" is useful. Providing your kids with a "no comment" answer is helpful. We are so tempted to give the media the true story, imagining that fair-minded people can make sense of your addiction and will quickly forgive you or be less angry with you. Unfortunately that is often not the case, at least in the beginning. In too many cases the media will distort the truth, omit crucial details, or slant the story in ways that will make you regret you said anything.

But make it possible for your children to play with their playmates, providing them with language to use to talk about the situation. For example, a 6 to 8-year-old child might say to a friend, "Some people said that my Daddy did some bad stuff. I don't know what happened and I don't want to talk about it. I love my Daddy and I don't want to talk about it. OK? If you keep talking about it, I have to go home."

Be supportive of your partner and children but allow them opportunities to vent their feelings. Listen, admit you have been wrong or agree that the media are not being fair or nice, and ask what you can do today to help them feel better. Even if your family members are not able to manage their own feelings during these times, manage your own emotional state in healthy ways. Vent your anger and sadness with your recovery peers and with your therapist, and develop ways to stay focused on helping your family in these high stress times.

Telling Neighbors or Members of Your Faith Community

Once the court situation is over, depending on the age of your children and following the tips in Chapter 6, be prepared to disclose and then provide ongoing information to help your youngsters cope with the situation. Decide on a need-to-know basis what to tell specific neighbors and those outside your immediate circle of family and best friends. Ask yourself:

- What do these people need to know to be able to interact with us without it being a problem?

- Will they hold this against my family? Will they let their children come over? Should their children be here, given your offense?

- What do you want to say about this disease, your behavior then and now, and the risk you are putting others in by being near them.

- If you have probation or parole requirements, what do the neighbors or others need to know about that to feel safer around you and your family?

- If the neighbors are being supportive, let them know what they can do to help. Inviting your children to their home for a fun activity or a sleepover can help your children feel some sense of normalcy. Perhaps they can sit with the children while you and your partner have an evening out or go for a walk together.

Sex Offender Registry

When an addict is listed on a sex offender registry, various types of disclosures are required. Most of the public believes that only pedophiles and rapists are listed on the registry. That is not true. A conviction of any sex offense can result in being placed on the registry, often with a legal description of the offense that is unclear about the behavior. For example, "sexual production with a minor" represents dozens of things, one of which might be what you did (such as made a video of yourself and a seventeen-year-old you thought was twenty-one), but your neighbors don't know that. In some states, judges even require sex offenders to put signs in their yards stating "Danger! A convicted sex offender lives here!" Preparing for being listed and handling people's reactions is important for the addict, partner, children, family, neighbors, and community.

Not every community is ready to support you if you have committed a sexual offense, but you may be surprised how people will support you if you are doing everything in your effort to stop your offending behavior and keep yourself and your community safe.

If you are on a registry or going to be, it is only a matter of time until someone finds out. First and foremost, your partner and children need to know how to handle the anger and fear of others. Excluding small children, everyone in the family needs to talk about the possibility of violence by uninformed, fearful, and angry people. You need to have your internal voice remind yourself that you are not bad (even if you did bad things) and you need to come from a place of strength, knowing that you have a right to be in your home, your yard. Still, it is important to be wise about what you do. Until you have a group in your community who knows some of your story and is supportive of your efforts to be healthy, it is wise to go places together. Being alone draws suspicion and a single person makes a better target than two or more. If you are single, then asking a friend to go with you to work out or to a movie allows you to be with someone. Explain to your friend what you will need to do if triggered or if your shame gets the best of you.

If you have been friendly with your neighbors in the past and none of them has been a victim of the offense, it is likely they will listen to what you have to say. What has worked best in these cases is to select one or two people or couples who are most likely to listen, learn, and be supportive. Ask those people to meet you in your home. When they are present tell them you have something very important you want to tell them and hope they will hear you out before making a judgment. A letter format works well here, too, as people usually will let you finish the letter before reacting or asking questions and getting distracted by their own confusion or fear. Of course, the addict should read this letter and the partner (or friend) should be present. If teenaged children are in the household, they can be present if they want the neighbors to know that they know and the family is working on this together.

The letter should:

1. Tell the purpose of the meeting.

2. Admit that you are guilty of the offense and that you will be listed or are already listed on the sex offender registry.

3. Admit that your actions were wrong and that you are sorry for hurting the victim, your family, them, and the community.

4. Declare that you are in therapy for the problem and are providing financial support for the victim to get therapy (if you are). If you are on probation, indicate that you have listed your probation officer's name and number on a card (that you give to them) should they want to report anything of concern or want to ask questions. (Check with your PO to determine that it is acceptable for them to receive these types of inquiries. They generally want neighbors to report anything suspicious.) Let them know the conditions of your probation (such as can't drink alcohol or be with minors unsupervised). If you have to move because you can no longer live in the household with your children, then explain the conditions under which you can see your children (Partner has to attend chaperone classes, can't be where there are other children, etc.).

5. Tell them that you want their support of your family. If you have children, indicate you don't want your children to be punished because of your behavior and want your children to be able to socialize with their children at their home. If it means that you can't participate in driving children to swim practice, admit you know it will mean more work for them, but you need their help to make sure your children aren't singled out to feel bad about something that was not their fault.

6. If they have children the same age as yours, indicate your willingness to discuss what to say to their kids about what has happened so the children are safe and not scared. Even when your offense doesn't involve children, people are afraid that you will progress to that. This is where sharing limited information about the nature of your offense is important. Outline what you are doing to make sure that you are not alone with children.

7. Again repeat that you are sorry for your actions and hope, after they think about it a while, they will be supportive of your children and your partner. At this point, if your partner and children want to, they may talk about how as a family everyone is working together to deal with this challenging time. Then ask if they have any questions or want to say anything.

8. If they are supportive, be grateful and agree to answer questions they might have. Most people want to be assured that their children are not at risk, so provide information about how that will be accomplished on an ongoing basis.

9. If they come down hard on you, agree that you have been wrong and only ask that they not hurt or punish your family because of your issues. Ask them to think about it and suggest that you all meet with your PO or therapist. (Again, seek approval from the PO or therapist prior to making that statement. Offer to pay your therapist for his or her time.)

Sometimes it is helpful to have this first conversation with your minister or rabbi or other religious leaders present in your home.

If you have been very isolated, it is less likely that your neighbors will be supportive. They have no history with you and will be afraid. Each case must be measured within the context of your situation.

We do know that people are less likely to re-offend or relapse if they are not isolated. So, whatever you do, find a place where you can share your situation. In most Sex Addicts Anonymous meetings you can talk about these issues.

Here is how the family of one sex offender handled the sex offender registry problem:

When Bill, a junior high school science teacher, was sentenced to twelve years in prison for having a sexual relationship with one of his fourteen-year-old students, his wife Colleen moved in with her parents in a quiet suburban neighborhood. Her parents helped with childcare of her three daughters while Colleen finished college, then graduate school, and became a successful career woman. Colleen's religion did not support divorce or remarriage, so Colleen decided to wait for her husband's release. Every week for twelve years Colleen and the children visited her husband in prison. She also arranged for a counselor to do joint counseling with the couple during additional prison visits.

Because Bill's arrest and conviction were widely reported in the newspapers, Colleen's neighbors were well aware of her circumstances. Over the years they got to know Colleen and her three daughters and came to admire her for her efforts to keep the family together. When it was time for Bill's release, Colleen visited each of the neighbors, beginning with the ones she knew were most supportive, and talked with them about Bill's approaching arrival, about how he had matured in prison and had spent years making amends to his family and regretting his offenses with the young student, and about the plans the family had to make a new life for themselves. She assured them that there were strict rules for Bill that did not permit him to be near their children or others and the actions he was taking to be in compliance with the conditions of his probation. She told them about the chaperone classes she had to take prior to his release and him moving back home. She assured them if by some chance one of their children saw him, he would wave and smile but that if they approached him he would say he had to go inside and could not visit. She asked to hear about any concerns they might have. By the time the neighbors were informed by law enforcement that a sex offender was about to live in their neighborhood, they were sufficiently knowledgeable about the situation that it was not a problem either for them or for Bill.

Colleen had for years dreamed about relocating to a new city, one where no-one had heard of Bill or his history, but she realized she would have the most support from the community if she stayed put. Her decision proved to be a good one.

Work Settings

Jason, a 42-year-old man with seven years of recovery from cocaine and sex addiction, landed a new job as marketing director of a psychiatric hospital. Surrounded as he was by psychotherapists, nurses, and other professionals sympathetic to people with psychological disorders, Jason soon disclosed to his co-workers his history of cocaine binges and anonymous sexual encounters and his Twelve-Step involvement. Unfortunately, the word quickly got up to the administrators of the hospital, who were less than pleased. One of them made Jason feel sufficiently uncomfortable that he soon moved on to another job. In his new position, he chose not to reveal his story.

If your acting out behavior doesn't impact your work setting, other than distracting you, then it is a private matter that is discussed with others primary in your life. However, if you are at risk of acting out at work or have previously done so on the job, you may need to disclose to someone in the workplace. If you are fairly certain that you will lose your job, then you have to weigh the importance of disclosure versus the impact of job loss on your recovery.

Sometimes the work setting is so filled with triggers that a relapse is likely if you continue to work there. It is not necessary to disclose if you are leaving your current job for one that is better suited for your recovery. What you divulge at work is determined by the likelihood of your boss or co-workers finding out and their need to know.

Here are some things to think about or discuss with your support group or therapist:

- How might your relapse prevention plan interfere with work or involve others?

- If you acted out at work, then who has been victimized by your behavior? Are amends in order?

- Is your work environment small enough that everyone needs to have at least some understanding about what you have done? Will that help them understand why you always bring up what you did with your wife over the weekend when an attractive female client enters the room?

- As a result of a higher authority (the court, licensure board, and sometimes your partner) are you required to only work with a certain population or stop working with a certain employee?

- Do new corporate policies and procedures need to be in place to protect the employees and management? What can you share that may help prevent problems in the future?

- To help you decide what if anything should be disclosed, you might want to complete a decision making matrix. Essentially, take a piece of typing paper and draw a large rectangle on it; then divide the rectangle into four smaller rectangles. In the upper-left rectangle, list positive consequences for disclosing, and in the upper-right rectangle list negative consequences for disclosing. In the bottom-left rectangle list positive reasons for not saying anything at work. In the lower-right rectangle, list negative reasons for not disclosing. Now review your responses. This should help you decide what to do.

For the most part, we advise that if people at work don't need to know, don't tell—unless it is vital for your recovery.

It is not always easy to balance the "rigorous honesty" of addiction recovery and the reality that disclosure in certain circumstances may have adverse consequences that call for careful planning or for silence. In this chapter we gave you guidelines for getting through this difficult experience. In the next chapter we will describe how to bring together what you have learned so far as you start your new life after disclosure.

Chapter Nine

After Disclosure – What Now?

After disclosure addicts report feeling relief at not having to live the double life, but they are also overwhelmed by the fear of the reactions to the pain they have inflicted. Partners are in shock, hurting beyond belief, and experiencing a wide range of emotions. Some partners are so overwhelmed they become depressed and suicidal, and isolate themselves due to the shame associated with the addict's behavior. Other partners feel threatened and are so angry they cannot tolerate having the addict near them; they often are quick to threaten divorce. The flood of emotions seems overwhelming and couples usually do not know what to do next. A rule of thumb for people early in recovery—do not make any major decisions in the first year.

To prevent further deterioration of the relationship, couples need to formulate a plan to keep the relationship on hold. Initially, it is useful to determine if you want a short separation. The idea is to separate so self-repair can be implemented and a support system can be established. The support system needs to both support you and hold you accountable. In volatile situations, having two places to live for a while is optimal.

Unfortunately, not everyone is in a position to do that. Even in situations in which people can manage their anger, sometimes they need a short time apart. Some homes are large enough so that each member of the couple can have their own private space to go to for self-repair. You may want to stay with friends or family for a few days. Learning to ask for help is a useful skill; this is a time to practice. However you decide to get your space, place a few things there that provide a sense of well-being. Sometimes it is helpful to print statements that represent how you want to think and respond—positive self-talk. This will help in times when you cannot easily remember how you want to respond to situations.

Boundaries and Agreements

To reduce further damage to the relationship, it is important to agree when you will talk with each other and how you will manage yourself during times when you are talking. If you feel that face-to-face discussions are too painful early on, then write notes to each other. If living separately, designate certain times to talk by phone or, if computer use is not an issue, correspond by email or texting. Because this is a cooling-off period, it is appropriate to decide what subject matter is off limits for now. For example, you may want to postpone intense discussions about the disclosure information until both of you have a support system in place and have had time to reflect about the impact of the addiction and trauma have had on your relationships, and most of all, on you.

It is important to talk about the acting-out behaviors, but we recommend you do that in therapy sessions. If that is not possible, delay the conversations until you've had some time to heal and get clear about your feelings and your hopes for the future.

When speaking about day-to-day issues, be careful not to fall into the trap of what John Gottman, Ph.D., who has studied married couples for years, calls the "Four Deadly Horsemen." Too often when couples are hostile with each other, they revert to four destructive styles of interacting. These do not always show up in this order, but generally the conversation starts in a harsh way. One party *criticizes* the other harshly rather than presenting a complaint. A complaint describes a specific behavior whereas a criticism contains harsh or negative words about your partner's personality, and frequently adds on some criticism from a previous situation unrelated to the specific behavior in question. For example, a complaint might be:

> *Len, I am frustrated because you agreed to pick up the kids from school and bring them home by 6:00 P.M., but you are consistently late.*

In contrast, a criticism would sound like this:

> *I cannot believe that you can't get this one thing right. What the hell is wrong with you? This is so simple; if you really cared you would get the kids back to me as we agreed. This is just like all the other times you've screwed up—no wonder I can't trust you.*

Another negative style is to use *contempt* when you complain or criticize. Sarcasm and cynicism are passive-aggressive ways to show contempt. They include mocking your partner, using hostile or inappropriate humor, being belligerent, rolling your eyes, and name calling—all of which send the signal that you are disgusted by your partner. Using contempt inevitably leads to more conflict or another "horseman"—stonewalling.

Stonewalling is when the listener gives the talker all the cues that he or she is not listening. There is no eye contact, no head nods, and no verbal encouragement—such as saying "uh-huh" or asking questions for clarification. The listener sits like a stone wall and looks down or away the whole time the other person is talking or goes to their room and shuts the door without explanation.

The fourth horseman is *defensiveness*. Defending your actions is a normal response when you are attacked, but in cases in which someone continues to criticize, defending yourself usually makes matters worse. This is especially true because as the addict you are the designated "bad guy" for now. When you defend yourself, you are saying the problem isn't me, it's you. Accountability is the first order of business for you during this phase. However, both the addict and partner have been in a dance of self-destructive behaviors and eventually you both have to learn to identify and change those behaviors, but for now, you have to accommodate more.

If you catch yourself using any of these styles, call a timeout and tell your partner you need a break for self-repair because you don't like the way you are thinking or behaving. One way to engage in self-repair is to learn to stay grounded internally.

Personal Healing: Self-Repair Through Internal Grounding

We want you to think about your authentic self. This is the person you strive to be—the healthy person in recovery. Your authentic self operates from a set of values that guide your behaviors. Below are some examples of values that would guide your behavior as an authentic person.

- A goal of all healthy people is to maintain a clear sense of their authentic selves. This is especially true when the heat gets turned up in a fight or when your brain gets hijacked by old memories. As you work though issues, you and your partner will become more and more important to each other. That makes the threat of losing your partner even more frightening. So when you call a time out for self-repair, remind yourself who you strive to be as an authentic person. Review your new values and tell yourself you refuse to return to presenting an inaccurate picture of yourself.

• Think about your anxieties, limitations, and shortcomings by identifying what is making you anxious or fearful. Determine what you can and cannot do. (Remember the Serenity Prayer – "God, grant me the serenity to accept the things I cannot change, courage to change the things I can, and wisdom to know the difference" —this is a good time to say it!) This will prevent your anxiety from driving your decisions or immobilizing you. I like to say another little prayer when I am stuck. "Help!" or the longer version is "Higher Power, I don't know exactly how to fix this. Please show me the way. If I can't fix it or if it isn't my job to fix it, help me to get through this with integrity and doing no harm."

• Hold yourself accountable. Identify what you are doing that is not helping the situation. Are you afraid? If so, are they reasonable fears about what is going on, or connected to something from your family of origin? Are you being selfish, trying to manipulate the situation, engaging in behaviors that you know will make things worse? What other options do you have that will make things better? What would you be doing if you really wanted to show your partner that you loved him/her?

• Acknowledge your projections and thinking errors. Admit when you are wrong—don't wait for your partner to do so first, or ever, for that matter.

• Tolerate the discomfort. It is the way to grow. Support yourself through positive affirmations. Pray for your partner. Soothe yourself through meditation, humming, or singing; have a special coloring book and color yourself to safety.

If this doesn't work at first, you just need some practice. Eventually you will find it will work for you. In the meantime, to create a safer playing field for discussions, the following guidelines may help:

- Be ready to call "time out for self-repair" if discussions become attack and defend games. Practice self-repair through the steps outlined above. Be sure to agree upon a time to continue talking later.

- To talk about painful issues, have an adult third person present if you are not able to have these discussions without becoming angry.

- When discussing, stick to the issues at hand until you get resolution or agree that you are stuck and need to cool off or get help before moving to another topic.

- Don't blame each other. Talk about feelings first. You may want to use the behavioral change request form outlined below in these discussions.

- If you cannot talk without getting out of control, agree to limit your contact to letters or emails or texts.

- Set specific hours you can be reached by phone.

If your separation is for more than a few days, establish ground rules for dealing with day-to-day responsibilities. Who will pay which bills? How will the needs of your children be met? If one parent is the primary care taker, how will respite and visitation be managed? What are the arrangements for visiting with the pets? Who will take the car to the tire repair shop? Initially, how long is the separation for? What do you need to demonstrate so your partner knows you are working your program of recovery?

To determine who should do what, make a list of all the things you were responsible for in day-to-day maintenance in your household. If logistics allow, it may be easier to keep doing what you have done. Otherwise, decide who is best at what. Additionally, if this is an area where the addict can "stretch" to show his commitment by handling new responsibilities, he might volunteer to take those on. Or if your partner has been an over-functioning partner, you might invite her to give up some of her responsibilities so you can demonstrate that you are totally committed to being more responsible.

If you have children, agree to treat each other like friends in front of them, no matter how angry or disappointed you are with yourself or your partner. You already know that it's not good for your children to be put in the middle of your pain, and have probably reproached yourself more than once for doing just that. If you can follow this suggestion, you will feel much better about yourself.

Regarding your sexual and emotional connection with your partner, often the partner has a list of "off-limits" items. This might include not being touched or kissed. Some partners don't want to be told that the addict loves them—others want to hear it and see behaviors that demonstrate this. Obviously, these items are an individual preference. Allowing your partner to have an "off-limits" list that you have to abide by may seem overly punitive to you, but during the first few weeks or months after disclosure, partners are frequently still in shock. It takes a while to even understand how she or he feels. Partners need a chance to get clarity about what the addictive behavior has done to affect life.

During the first year when your partner complains or gets caught in her post-traumatic stress by remembering events of the past, it is especially helpful for you to acknowledge that what you did was wrong. Reassure her that she has every right to feel the way she does. After you acknowledge your past behaviors, you can help your partner stay in the present by asking her what you can do today to improve things. Is there any way to stop the pain and to feel better? The pain is part of the grieving process; there is no way around it unless you stuff your pain, which is not a good idea. For several weeks, set aside a time every few days to note what impact the addiction has had on you so that you can share that information with your group, therapist, or close friend. It is through talking about what has happened and listening that we grow, understand, and heal. It is important for you and your partner to share what you are learning about yourself through recovery, so find a time to do that.

Managing Emotional States

As you can see, the process of disclosure is an opportunity to "grow yourself up" or mature in ways that help you personally and help your relationship. It is your responsibility for your own healing. In times of crisis, we often mismanage our emotions and make matters worse. Someone who is able to manage emotional states is said to have high emotional intelligence. According to Daniel Goleman (2006) that means the person can:

- Recognize a feeling as it happens.

- Manage emotions by soothing yourself and bounce back quickly from life's challenges and minor crises.

- Motivate self to have self-control in order to delay gratification and control impulses.

- Recognize emotions in others and have empathy for them.

- Manage your own emotional state when the other person can't manage his or her own emotions.

Emotions that are most often mismanaged are anger, fear, shame, and power. The emotional state that encourages mismanaged anger the most is shame. Shame is guilt's big brother. Guilt is feeling awful for having gone too far or for not having done enough. Shame is feeling inadequate for not being worthy enough. Underlying shame are confusion and a feeling of abandonment. Shame makes us want to either blame someone so we don't have to look at our part in the situation or get revenge for how someone hurt us. But getting revenge doesn't mean getting over what has happened. Also, getting revenge never feels very good for long. Instead, it builds a wall around us that doesn't allow healing love to penetrate.

Anger can be helpful to give us energy, but after a while it gets in the way of healing. Because of the intensity of the feeling, we are seduced into believing that the anger is making us stronger when it actually can diminish our personal power. When we mismanage anger we get caught up in the obsession of the events surrounding the betrayal and we relive the pain of the disclosure over and over. If this goes unchecked we continue to feel powerless. And that is a move right back to addictive and co-addictive behavior.

When we mismanage any emotion, it is often related not only to the current situation but some past event as well. For example, most people have experienced some type of childhood trauma. Birth, after all, is traumatic. But even in the best of families, natural events occur: pets die, teachers or coaches can be harsh, in some families children are expected to do far more than is reasonable. Others are sexually or physically abused. Unless a caring adult is around to help a young person make sense of what has happened, the child will make up stories in his or her mind about why and how something happened—usually taking the blame for things going bad. This self-blame then becomes the way the person sees traumatic events that happen in the present. In other words, the events of today are experienced with the eyes and emotions of the child who was traumatized earlier in life. The person stays stuck in the past and mismanages the emotional state of the present

Learn from the Past, Stay in the Present

One way to "grow yourself up" is to learn from the past and stay in the present. Anytime you feel that past emotions may be interfering with taking appropriate action in the present, below are some steps you can take:

1. What am I feeling right now?

2. What does this remind me of?

3. What feelings are underneath what I am experiencing now? (Under anger we often find fear and sadness.)

4. How can I best express my feelings to maximize healing and grow?

5. Do I need to hold someone accountable or am I over-reacting because this reminds me of the past? (If it is reminding me of the past, is there someone from my past I need to hold accountable?)

6. What is my part in helping to create the situation?

7. What can I learn from the situation?

8. How am I powerful in the situation?

9. How do I want to transition to another place in the relationship with myself and my partner?

Once you are able to really figure out what is happening in a given situation, you can then take appropriate action. Instead of mismanaging an emotional state to put distance between you, hold yourself and the other person accountable. Remember also that you are most powerful when you can come from love instead of anger or fear.

How to Hold Someone Else Accountable

1. Write a detailed description of the event or situation about which you experience pain, anger, or another powerful feeling.

2. What meaning did you give to the event? How did you interpret the other person's behavior? (This is a great exercise to teach to kids as well.)

3. How did you make matters worse for yourself?

4. What do you want the other person to do today to help you to heal?

Re-read this again and determine if you are calm enough to discuss this with the other person. If so, ask for an appointment to share this important information. Otherwise return to self-soothing activities until you are managing your emotional discomfort.

If your partner or another person has asked you to be accountable and you feel defensive in response, then you will want to follow the steps listed below. Remember, being defensive doesn't work.

Holding Myself Accountable

1. Repeat what you heard about what you did that your partner or someone is asking you to be accountable for.

2. Acknowledge that what you did had an impact on the other person. Look for ways in which this person has a good point and agree with anything you can.. (You can always agree that she (or he) seems upset and after hearing her description and the meaning to her, you can tell her you understand how she would feel that way.)

3. Humbly state you are sorry and ask for forgiveness.

4. If this person has requested something of you, tell her if you can fulfill her request. If not, suggest a few other options you can do.

Sometimes we use the "behavioral change request" activity in the same way. It is a common communication exercise that many therapists recommend, but has a built-in accountability clause for you as well.

Behavior Change Request

Use this exercise any time you need to talk to your partner about a sensitive issue. It holds both of you accountable for your parts in the situation. Until it becomes easy, write the answers to each line, and then ask your mate for time to process.

1. I feel frustrated when you _____

2. Other emotions I feel are _____

3. I make matters worse by _____

4. To hide my fear that _____

5. I also feel sad about _____

6. What I really want from you today to make this better is _____

7. What I expect of myself in this situation is _____

Distrust and suspiciousness are to be expected in the early stages after disclosure. Although some therapists may recommend doing some detective work to diminish the fears of the partner, we find this type of behavior often consumes the energy of the partner and produces a probation officer/offender relationship for the couple. This keeps the addict and partner on unequal footing, which is often a trigger for both parties to resume old behaviors.

Sometimes the partner can't get unstuck from obsessing about the addict's past behaviors and projects them on everything that happens in the present. Often an addict will offer to take a polygraph test in her presence, if that will help. Sometimes just offering to do this "objective" measure is enough insurance or proof to the partner that she can move on with her work. Our research has shown that when the addicted person undergoes a polygraph test as part of his or her relapse prevention and as a way to reassure the partner, the polygraph results are usually seen as helpful to both the partner and addict.

Similarly, the drug addict may be asked to submit to a urine drug screen, which is a test for various drugs of abuse in a urine specimen. This test is routinely used in physician monitoring programs and in other recovery situations. A series of negative results (i.e., no illicit substances are found in the urine) establishes a track record of recovery; some addicts find it useful to have this outside monitoring until they learn to manage their emotions rather than act out.

Rebuilding Trust

One of the most devastating consequences of disclosure of secrets is the loss of trust experienced by the partner. Of course, it is a mistake to consider the cause of the loss of trust to be the disclosure—that is only the precipitating factor; it is analogous to blaming the messenger for the bad news. *The underlying causes of the loss of trust are the addict's behavior and the lies that were used to cover it up.* Words and promises will not do it—changed behaviors and evidence of honesty are the keys to rebuilding trust.

Your partner has to believe that you have the intention to change for her to begin to trust again. More importantly, your partner has to believe you have the competency to implement the changes. A partner may believe an addict wants to change but she may not think he can do it. She will not trust him again until she is convinced he has the skill to do what he says he intends to do. A commonly heard complaint by addicts is, "I've been toeing the line for six weeks, yet my partner says she can't trust me as far as she can throw me. I'm no longer engaging in my addictive behavior, I come home early every day or phone my wife if I'm delayed, I participate in therapy and self-help groups. What more do I have to do?" The answer is, more of the same, for another year or two. It doesn't seem fair, but think about how long you have been acting out. For most addicts, comparatively, a couple of years is not much. Rebuilding trust after disclosure of a serious transgression is a process, one that takes an average of two years according to research on recovering couples. (Schneider & Schneider, 1999). At six weeks, the process is only beginning.

Here are some criteria by which trust is evaluated. Think about what you can do to ensure your evaluation is a good one.

1. **Be Honest**. You practice no deception, you don't lead a secret life apart from your partner, and you don't tell lies or omit the truth when you talk about events with others. Addicts become so accustomed to lying that it becomes second nature. You frequently lie, even about matters where there is no reason to lie and no cost to telling the truth. After years of watching you lie, dissemble, stretch and bend the truth, and cover up various actions, it's not surprising your partner does not trust you. You have to build a new track record to combat the miserable one that your partner has had much experience observing. One of the most effective trust-rebuilding strategies for the addict is to adopt a lifestyle of rigorous honesty. For example, if your partner asked you to pick up a carton of milk on the way home and you forgot, your previous approach upon arrival home might have been to tell her, "I got held up at the office and didn't have time," or some other such excuse. Instead, try telling the truth: "I'm so sorry, it just slipped my mind." If the two of you are shopping at the hardware store and the clerk gives you an extra dollar bill in change, give it back. When your partner observes you being honest in the small ways day after day, week after week, she will be more likely to believe that you will be honest in the big ways.

2. **Be Transparent**. This means your life is an open book to your partner and that you both have the same goals regarding your life together and for healing as a couple. You seek to understand your partner, to know him or her better so that you can respond to her or his needs when asked. When your partner requests information from you, you are totally forthcoming.

3. **Be Accountable**. You do what you say or promise and you have proof of what you say. That means any activity you have with another person can be verified. You are no longer vague or unreachable. It may even mean that you give your accountability buddy permission to speak to your partner about matters of concern to her or him. Let your partner tell you when you are providing too much information in your attempts to be accountable, especially in the first year. Over time, as trust builds, you both will get into a rhythm – but do not get lazy.

Taking your recovery for granted will lead to slips, and slips will lead to relapse if you don't increase your trust factors.

4. **Be Ethical**. Make your standards high for yourself. Have integrity in all you do. Be fair.

5. **Build An Alliance**. We know that family, specifically partners play an important role in helping get people to take steps towards recovery. After a betrayal, it is difficult for partners to believe you will ever be trustworthy enough to trust again but partners want their mate to "have their backs". Your partner wants you on her or his side – and you want her on your side. That is what trust is about. Being on your partner's side means that your partner has evidence that you no longer operate out of self-interest and you do not form coalitions against her. You have your partner's best interest at heart.

These criteria are based on the work of John Gottman (2011) in his book *The Science of Trust*. He also points out that for couples to really heal they must work toward more equality within the relationship. Early on this is difficult. The more you can replace conflict avoidance with constructive conflict management, the greater your chances of feeling more equal in the relationship.

While you have heard repeatedly in this book that you and your partner need to work on your individual recovery, we need to remind you that for your relationship to be satisfying and long lasting, your commitment should include working towards interdependence. Counting on each other to get your central needs met, building new goals together, and utilizing more positive self-talk about the relationship help to strengthen the relationship. It is important to cherish your partner, instead of trash her/him; to be grateful for this journey rather than resentful for the amount of work and pain that has to be endured. This is a gradual process.

Ending A Relationship

No matter how hard you try, in some cases, the relationship doesn't get better, the partner nor the addict seem to get better. The couple falls back into old patterns of relating, partners remain critical and addicts remain defensive. It seems easier to keep up the fight or just submit and withdraw. There is no a mutuality of needs, emotional need is not processed, and the hurt doesn't heal. Rather than turning towards each other to try to solve problems, there is turning away and no restoration of trust. In these cases, to get better the addict and partner have to end their destructiveness by ending the relationship. Sometimes this is clear early on; other times it takes years.

If it does happen, then it is important to grieve the loss. Perhaps it is the loss of the fantasy that one day you would have a happy, satisfying relationship. Perhaps it is the loss of your children for long periods of time. It can be loss over many things, but it is still important to understand the impact the loss has on you. Seek help to talk about the pain and anger (and other emotions that will be generated due to the loss). Start new rituals for holidays and vacations with recovering friends. Realize that you can still treat your partner in friendly ways and above all, have integrity about what you do. That is part of your recovery.

Recommitment

After a lot of hard work and self-searching, most couples want to reconcile and recommit to their relationship. This is after caring has been re-established through relationship-enhancing behaviors. Research tells us that the prognosis is good for couples in which both are committed to making the journey of recovery together (Gordon & Baucom, 2003). True intimacy starts after you learn how to trust yourself and manage your emotions in healthy ways rather than fall back into old ways of thinking and acting.

Couples who survive the first two years or so of recovery are surprised at how strong they have become as individuals. They are ready to recommit to having a marriage that is realistic and a healthy place to grow as individuals. Research indicates that couples who stay together and report long-term happiness have goals for their relationship in addition to goals for individual growth. They have established caring, commitment, and a process of compassionate communication. We know how terrible your emotional pain has been. Our hope is that now you are on the way to true friendship with your partner.

Stay Positive

It is difficult to stay positive when all this pain and shame that is occurring. As part of your daily inventory, make sure you identify something that you are grateful for right now. Also remember your strengths and achievements, not just your challenges. Remember what the faces look like of five people who love you, warts and all.

Hang around with positive people. Author and popular motivational speaker, Tommy Newberry (2007) shares a visual example he uses with teens about choosing friends wisely. While on stage he gets a volunteer to let Tommy try to pick him up onto the stage using just one arm. After some exaggerated attempts with no success, he then invites the young person to try to pull him down from the stage just using one finger – an easier task. The audience quickly gets the message – it is far easier to be pulled down than lifted up. This is especially true early in recovery. What we have also learned from research with recovering people is that when people who have good recovery hang out together, they tend to stay sober longer, and to be happier.

So be alert to who is lifting you up and who is pulling you down. Look for people whose integrity is high, who share you values about recovery, and demonstrate joyful living. Look for those who will also bring the best out in you and will challenge you to honor your recovery principles. And finally, rather than only being grateful about getting something that is missing, try appreciating what you are presented with. Life is as easy as we make it.

References

Bader, Ellen, and Pearson, Paul. *In Quest of the Mythical Mate*. New York: Brunner Mazel.1988.

Glass, Shirley. 2001, personal communication

Goleman, Daniel. *Emotional Intelligence*. New York: Bantam Books, 2006.

Gottman, John. *Why Marriages Succeed or Fail*. New York: Simon & Schuster, 1994.

Gottman, John. *The Science of Trust*. New York: Norton, 2011.

Gordon, K. C. & Baucom, D. H. (2003). Forgiveness and marriage. American Journal of Family Therapy, 31, 179–199.

Newberry, Tommy. *The 4:8 Principle: The Secret to a Joy-filled Life.* Carol Stream, IL: Tyndale House Publishers, Inc., 2007.

Schneider, J. and Schneider, B.H. *Sex, Lies, and Forgiveness: Couples Speak on Healing from Sex Addiction,* Third Edition, Tucson, Ariz.: Recovery Resources Press, 2005.

SIECUS Report, Washington DC: Sex Information and Education Council of the United States, 1995.

Chapter Ten

For Helping Professionals

Because disclosure of sexual information tends to be the most difficult for professionals to handle, this chapter refers to working with sexual infidelity. The information provided is appropriate to most addictive behavior.

Relationship distress in couples in which a disclosure or discovery of extramarital behavior has occurred frequently motivates one or both members of the couple to seek professional help. Because this type of disclosure is taken so personally by the partner, we have added this chapter for professionals helping couples deal with revelations of a sexual nature. The guidelines outlined in this chapter are appropriate for other types of disclosures as well.

There are many similarities between non-addicted and addicted couples seeking help to work through the labyrinth of emotions and decisions. However, there are several special needs of the addict. The therapist's actions can be instrumental in helping both the individual and the couple make progress towards healing.

Differences between Addicted and Non-addicted Couples

Almost all unfaithful mates struggle with disclosure. As with addicts, they do not want to hurt their partners nor get into trouble, so their tendency is to avoid opening up. Yet, most of the books on surviving infidelity promote honesty about the behavior (mostly affairs). This makes sense because the majority of these books are authored by women who have survived an affair. Most men or women who have had an affair would prefer that they did not have to disclose. Unfortunately, guilt or evidence often prompts telling. In addition to the unfaithful mate's guilt, there exists a wide range of emotions for both people in the relationship.

We have little information about the number of people who get involved in affairs, or go on sexual binges of some type outside the primary relationship and if not caught, do not tell. In the past, several prominent public figures were caught being unfaithful and made matters worse by denying their involvement with an affair partner or their extensive cybersex or pornography use. In the more recent past, many of these high-profile cases have started with early admission in hopes of cooling down the media frenzy. While that seems like progress, anyone paying attention to the partner of these (mostly) men, some of whom stand dutifully at their husband's side as he publicly divulges his transgression can see from their body language that they are in distress.

Why, then, do we promote disclosure for addicts and their partners? Partly because of the outcome of our research: Most addicts and partners agree that telling was useful and in most cases helped them stay sober, gave them enough hope to stay involved in each other's lives in healthy ways, and demonstrated the motivation to change.

Another very important reason is because addictive behaviors are repetitive in nature. Being addicted means that your brain is formatted to seek out situations in which the brain chemistry will be altered enough to ensure an altered mood. The majority of addicts cannot manage to gain any health if they are still sexually involved outside the relationship—they experience too much shame and guilt, which are strong stimuli for relapse. Just as an alcoholic cannot hang out in a bar and expect to abstain from alcohol, sex addicts cannot hang out where their "drug" of choice is, without risking acting out again. Most addicts and partners find that honesty helps them remain connected to their recovery efforts. Disclosure seems to offer hope—and almost a form of insurance for the addict and his or her partner. To lie or continue to lie just fuels the engine that runs the addiction and further traumatizes the partner.

Therefore, we do encourage addicts to come clean to their mates (and vice-versa) in almost all cases. On the other hand, if someone is not an addict, we examine the context and meaning of the infidelity before making any recommendation about disclosure. If a client requests guidance about whether to reveal an affair, some questions worthy of discussion in individual therapy session are:

- Is the affair over?

- Does the client still have any contact with the affair partner, or does his or

- her spouse?

- Does the client still have strong emotions about the affair partner?

- How did the affair impact the couple's relationship?

- What lies were used to cover up the affair?

- Did the partner suspect, and if so, how much energy and additional lying was necessary to disarm the partner's suspicions? (For example, was the partner accused of imagining things, paranoia, etc. that perhaps contributed to the partner's loss of self-esteem?)

- Is this the only affair the client has had, or has this been a recurring pattern?

- Does the past affair have any impact on the couple's current relationship?

- How comfortable does the client feel about continuing to conceal the affair?

- What is the meaning for the client of continuing not to disclose, and of disclosing?

- What does the client believe will be the positive as well as negative consequences of revealing the affair (on himself, on the spouse, on the relationship)?

- What does the client believe will be the positive and negative consequences of continuing not to divulge the affair (on himself, on the spouse, on the relationship)?

By clarifying the reasons for the client's consideration of disclosure, you can help him or her decide if it would be the right thing to do. By asking about other affairs, you may be able to identify an addiction problem, in which case telling is recommended, and may itself constitute an intervention that will lead to addiction treatment for the unfaithful spouse.

If your client is someone in a committed relationship or marriage who suspects her or his mate of infidelity, you need to consider in your differential diagnosis the possibility that her (or his) mate is a sex addict who has repeatedly lied to her. If she complains that her mate's interest in sex with her has diminished, consider that he may be getting his sexual needs met in other ways. If you are seeing both partners, keep in mind that the possibility that one is keeping secrets from the other, and make it clear to each client in advance what you will do if one of them reveals to you secrets that he or she is keeping from the other. We will discuss these issues below.

Before even embarking on this discussion, however, it is important to be aware of your own bias. We recommend that you ask yourself the following questions:

- Have you (the therapist) had an extramarital affair yourself, or have you been the betrayed partner?

- How does your personal experience about affairs, secrets, and lies affect your feelings and beliefs about the appropriateness of the client's disclosing the affair?

Understanding your own feelings about disclosure will allow you to counsel the client more objectively and more effectively.

The Role of the Therapist

As a therapist, it is not your role to side with either the partner or the addict. It is tempting to side with the partner because the addict has done the betraying. However, this puts the therapist in a triangulated position and allows the couple to focus on blaming or proving their point through the therapist rather than dealing with their own issues within the context of the relationship. Early in therapy, the couple looks to the therapist as the all-knowing expert. Sharing information about what you have learned through the literature, research, and your own clinical experience with couples dealing with addiction can be useful in order to give the couple hope and help them be realistic about what to expect.

The therapist helps to interpret what is happening and discusses the differences between how men and women view and interpret situations. She or he validates each one's reality and the intensity of their feelings. As a coach, the therapist offers strategies to help the couple communicate more effectively (especially the listening and reflecting part of communicating). Incorporating cognitive behavioral exercises will help correct thinking errors and develop skills to build emotional competence. Personal responsibility can be enhanced by teaching the couple skills for holding self and each other accountable.

As the couple progresses you will see them able to move from the attack-defend mode of interacting to productively handling disagreements or difficult issues. Gradually, they will address problems without blaming or bringing up past betrayals. Having moved from interventionist in the early crisis phase, to educator and then coach during the rebuilding stage, the therapist's role near the end of therapy changes to cheerleader, letting the couple practice what they have learned.

How Long in Therapy

Working with these couples is a long-term commitment on everyone's part. It takes between two and five years for recovery to really get integrated into the lives of the couple. Couples therapy helps the relationship grow and sustain the stormy times. We have found that couples most often enter therapy for at least twelve weeks, make progress, and then come back bi-monthly, then monthly for the first year. We typically see couples for monthly maintenance or as crises arise. Couples can benefit from support groups through their local church or synagogue or Recovering Couples Anonymous (see Appendix 2).

Crisis Intervention and Early Therapy

Your introduction to a couple often begins with a telephone call from the partner, who reports a crisis—his infidelity. Ask her when and how she found out, and if there has been an ongoing problem regarding sex in the marriage. If the addict calls, it is usually because the partner has discovered something about his sexual activities, and a major disruption of the marriage has resulted. Ask if the addict thinks he has a serious problem, if he has sought help for the problem and if so, is he still in therapy. Determine if he is still acting out. If yes, then schedule an individual session to assess his commitment to getting into recovery.

The partner is usually in a state of shock, either full of rage and anger or devastated and hopeless. She may vacillate between these emotional states, become anxious, and phone you day and night, weekends and holidays. While listening to her is vital to the process, your ability to model some healthy boundary-setting is equally as important. Assure her that some feelings of desperation and chaos are normal for this period and help her develop a plan for coping with them, including postponing calling you until a designated time. Help her identify a support system by recommending S-Anon, COSA, or Al-Anon meetings (see Appendix 2 for support groups) and clarifying with her who may be safe to share this information with.

In the first few sessions (or in those frantic phone calls) it is helpful to reduce her fear by validating her experience and reassuring her that she is not crazy and that self-care is of the utmost importance. Help her establish obtainable goals in these areas.

In our study, most respondents did see a therapist. In fact, most saw more than one. The partners reported that the most important and useful part of seeing a therapist was being supported and feeling heard. Specifically, several partners commented that helpful therapists established a safe atmosphere in which they felt free to ask questions at any time and in which their suspicions were validated. Partners indicated that the therapists allowed them to make choices.

The second valuable type of advice was to take care of themselves and to recognize that the addict's behavior was not the partner's fault. Partners told us it was helpful for them to be told to give yourself time and space to heal, not to make rash decisions, how to set boundaries, and that self-worth comes from inside, not from other people.

In contrast, addicts reported that the most useful advice was what and how to tell. Some (60%) thought that advice to be honest and tell everything was the most useful. Rather than demand that the addict disclose, a persistent, gentle coaching to share information with the partner was seen as the most motivating. The therapist discouraged keeping secrets, warning that secrets are destructive and severely damage trust. Therapists also helped addicts make better choices by considering many options. Most often though, respondents reported the most useful advice was that honesty is the best way to rebuild the relationship

Help the addict identify his values and formulate ideas about how honesty can be helpful to him in his relationship with his partner and his recovery. Have him be specific about setting goals for honesty.

Although most people in our study reported their experience with advice from therapists to be satisfactory, those who responded to the question about least helpful advice spoke of the impact and seriousness of disclosure for both the addict and the partner. The primary negative theme identified for both addict and partner was lack of knowledge and skill by the therapist. This included lack of responsiveness to the emotional condition of the partner. Below are some comments by partners that illustrate the seriousness of the situation for the partner:

> *Another therapist counseled my husband and me, but she didn't know that it was an addiction. Instead, she encouraged me to be a better sexual partner and support his habits.*

> *When I found out my husband prefers men or children, I was really devastated. My self-esteem was shaky and that finished it off. I was afraid for my children. I didn't think my husband would stay in our home. Months later my psychiatrist told me he was a pedophile— by then I was so depressed I was planning to kill myself and my children.*

> *I was so angry, but isolated. I needed to talk about my feelings, but his behavior was all we could see. Maybe disclosure should follow preparation. This was such a dangerous time for me.*

> *The first two therapists did not address my need to ask more. I saw a psychologist for a period of time. He was ill-prepared to help me. He questioned my aversion to knowing the details. It confused me.*

> *I felt I let my children down enormously by dragging them through all the sordid details. Early, I should have been cautioned about who I disclosed to and advised to connect up with S-Anon groups. I acted inappropriately by making several phone calls to two women he'd been with.*

Obviously from these comments, the serious nature of the emotional state of the partners was not enough of a concern for the therapist. Assess the emotional state of the partner before moving forward with further disclosure or before letting the partner leave after a difficult session. Establish a firm goal with her about safety and check for suicidal ideation.

To further assess the case, it can be helpful to give each client a take-home questionnaire at the end of the first session. Questionnaires can be helpful not only to gain information, especially with sexual addiction cases, but as a means of letting each partner "vent." Ask about the type and level of current disruption, abuse during childhood, sexual history including other outside sexual and emotional involvement prior to marriage, sexual behavior and satisfaction within the marriage, other marital satisfaction issues, and how the couple attempts to enhance the relationship. Maintain strict confidentiality about information in the forms. If you determine that some information contained in the questionnaire needs to be shared with the spouse, work with the individual to come to that decision. It is much more useful for the client to realize that himself or herelf rather than for you to demand it. If the homework is not completed, it may be a sign of no privacy at home or a lack of commitment to the process by one or both parties.

After trust has been broken, couples often struggle with what to do about the marriage. It is common to see the partner beset with fear that she will be hurt again or will not be able to heal from the betrayal. She is likely to threaten to leave, want him out of the house, leave herself, or become so hypervigilant that she becomes obsessed by his every move. Reassure couples that their ambivalence and fear about the future of the relationship is normal at this stage. Establish an agreement to not do anything about leaving for three to six months. We recommend waiting a year, but most couples have a difficult time postponing this decision for what seems like such a lengthy time. Couples in early recovery are usually more comfortable agreeing to sit tight for three to six months, and then reassess where they are. At that time, they can recommit to continuing to work on their marriage and perhaps increase their level of commitment to each other. You should also recognize, and advise the couple, that the real recovery takes between two and five years.

Our research and experience indicate that rarely does an addict reveal all during the initial disclosure. He is either afraid of the outcome so only tells what he thinks is enough to get by, or he doesn't remember all his acting out and the lies he told to cover up his actions.

Reiterate to the couple that more than one disclosure is probable and set up a system by which past events can be discussed. To deal with the likelihood that the addict will eventually remember more material or may gradually come to recognize the need to acknowledge additional matters, agree on a schedule of perhaps once per month for the first three to six months for further revelation of past events and discussion of how the addiction has impacted both their lives.

Addiction is a chronic, relapsing condition; it takes time for the addict to learn to manage it. The partner needs to understand this, and to create a plan proactively for self-care, should a setback take place. If the addict has a slip or relapse, new disclosures should be done as soon as possible. Keeping the information secret will only make the partner trust the addict less. In our most recent research on disclosure of relapse, in couples where the addict admitted the relapse before the partner discovered it, both reported greater satisfaction in the relationship and higher levels of trust.

Recognize that despite preparation, any further disclosure is a setback for the partner. Nonetheless, if she can avoid punishing the addict for being honest, this will increase his level of emotional confidence and be empowering for her. If he continues to relapse, she may have to re-evaluate her desire to stay in a marriage in which the person will not use the tools he has been taught to keep himself healthy.

Early on, suggest that the addict clear the home of as many triggers and paraphernalia as possible. Careful attention to this can be a powerful statement to the partner that the addict is serious about changing. For example, if online sexual activities were part of his repertoire before recovery, the addict can move the computer to a public area in the household, purchase "parental control" software that will block access to sexually oriented Web sites, give the password to a 12-step sponsor or friend, and create accountability by "book-ending" his use of the Internet (that is, phone a program friend or sponsor immediately before and after using the computer).

Before the advent of laptops, iPads, Smartphones, and other mobile devices, when computer access took place either at home or in the workplace, strategies to restore trust involved only the home computer. These are still useful, but no longer enough. Suggest to the addict that he discuss with his partner ways of reassuring her that he is not using his portable electronic device to connect with other partners, view pornography, or engage in other activities that were part of his previous acting out. One way is to purchase and install blocking software that can function not only on your home computer but also on multiple mobile devices. Software websites will inform you if their product is appropriate for your devices. A good resource for comparing various products is www.sexualrecovery.com/online-controls-for-sex-romance-addicts.php. Some software provides accountability; that is, an "accountability partner" is notified if the user attempts to visit websites that are blocked, uses the GPS function on his mobile device, and various other activities. The accountability partner may be the therapist, a Twelve-Step sponsor, or a supportive friend. It is not a good idea to use the addict's partner as his accountability partner, especially early on when the partner is traumatized and reactive. Putting the partner in a parental, monitoring role can adversely affect the couple relationship.

Explain to the addict that these strategies not only reassure the partner, but they also actually protect the addict and help prevent slips. They can be viewed as the equivalent of a recovering alcoholic taking the drug Antabuse (disulfiram). If alcohol is ingested by a person who has this drug in his body, he will experience headache, nausea, vomiting, chest pain, anxiety, and other unpleasant symptoms. Thus, the drug serves as a deterrent to the alcoholic who might otherwise take a drink on impulse.

Most partners want to know why the addict did what he did. Rather than focus on the why, it is more beneficial for the couple to talk about the meaning of the addictive behavior to each of them. How to do a formal disclosure is outlined earlier in the book. Once the anger and fear have subsided, discuss what aspects of the relationship are sources of emotional distress for the partner or addict. Explore with the couple alternative ways of viewing those situations or other ways to interact during those times. Also make plans for dealing with other high-risk times such as work difficulties, financial hardships, accidents, or illnesses. Be certain the couple recognizes that anniversary dates of the disclosure or discovery or other particularly painful events can be difficult occasions. These anniversaries tend to re-ignite the partner's anger and the addict's shame; they need to be planned for appropriately. The couple needs to increase their ability to cope with emotional distress in general and have firm plans for those anniversary dates.

Inability to manage intimacy is often paradoxically seen after a particularly loving or pleasurable time together. Whichever member of the couple is least able to tolerate closeness will re-establish distance through conflict or by ignoring the other. The resulting confusion creates mismanaged fear, which then becomes a trigger for either addictive or codependent acting out. Resuming sexual intimacy also may trigger flashbacks in the partner. Predict the likelihood of these phenomena and co-create strategies with the couple to help them manage.

More intense flashbacks and other post traumatic symptoms in the partner can throw the couple into another crisis. Intrusions by a former affair partner, an anniversary date, the discovery of old acting out paraphernalia, or the exposure of a lie to the partner about an important event trigger obsessive thoughts for the partner. The addict's best defense is to agree his past behavior was wrong, express sorrow, and then ask if there is anything he can do now to remedy the situation. It is the therapist's task in session to help the partner get unstuck. Ask her to identify any additional unanswered questions and to recognize if she is mismanaging an emotional state. Encourage her to express pain without blaming. Advise her to set aside specific times for obsessing, to use a thoughts/feelings journal to help her identify thinking errors, and to develop plans of action. Meditation and prayer are also helpful for most people. Some therapists have found it helpful to use EMDR (eye movement desensitization and reprocessing) to reprocess and extinguish the power of traumatic memories of the betrayal.

It is common for one or both of the parties to have other addictions, depression, or anxiety. Both partners need to address and begin treatment of any other addictive behavior. If severe depression and anxiety are present, consider referral to a psychiatrist for prescription medication. However, remember that some depression and anxiety is normal; it is important for the client to learn to manage those emotional states rather than medicate them away.

If the couple decides to end the marriage, then the goal of therapy is to gain closure and determine what, if any relationship, they want to have with each other. If they share children, help them to negotiate how to manage the responsibilities of co-parenting.

Beginning Repair Work

We have outlined a number of activities for couples to begin the healing process. Encourage the couple to talk about what gives them hope for the future and brainstorm ways in which they can engage in relationship-enhancing behaviors. Most couples can recall some of the early fond memories of their relationship to rekindle these good feelings. Have them talk about how they fell in love in the first place and what attributes attracted each of them to the other. If the couple expresses resistance to this approach, have them focus instead on how they'd like their relationship to be now. Ask them to list the qualities of a best friend and to decide what they want to do differently each day to demonstrate that they are the other's best friend. In Chapter 9 we reviewed several ways to have the addict work toward rebuilding trust. Checklists of how things have improved are very useful.

Most couples have engaged in dysfunctional patterns of attack-defend, pursue-distance, nag-procrastinate, and blame-placate. Children or in-laws are often triangulated into these patterns of interacting that reduce or create homeostasis within the relationship. Couples who learn to relate directly can enhance their time together.

People in recovery often devote so much time and effort on recovery activities that couples forget to go on dates with each other or to spend some alone time together. Encourage them to set aside time to be together to either talk or just to enjoy each other's company. Suggest a homework assignment in which partner and addict alternate in asking for the date, selecting the location, and even driving to and paying for the date.

Encourage open discussion in session of the couple's sexual relationship. As mentioned earlier, this often will provoke flashbacks and difficult times. After a period of hard work, it is particularly useful for the couple to plan a special occasion in which to declare their renewed commitment and trust with each other. Discuss how to optimize sex for both partners. Rather than focus on what behaviors are off-limits, have the partner determine first what affectionate, loving, and sexual behaviors she is open to.

After that time, we recommend that couples schedule "intimacy times." If sex happens, fine. If not, we encourage holding each other, kissing, and other forms of intimacy. These activities can be particularly fulfilling when they are part of the couple's date night.

After couples have been in therapy and recovery for several years, the partner is ready to engage in additional sexual behaviors that both might enjoy, but which may feel more risky to one or the other. Frequently, the addict may hesitate to request a particular sexual act for fear that the partner will think he wants to act out. Encourage couples to dialogue about their sexual desires and to explore whether this is an option. Reading aloud from a recommended book on sexuality (*Erotic Intelligence* by Alex Katehakis is one we recommend) is a great way for couples to discuss whether they would want to participate in a behavior or not. However, if the addict has used the partner as a way to act out, these couples need to first process extensively with each other the meaning of sexual expression.

Special Areas of Concern for Therapists

Below we discuss some special areas of concern for therapists who are counseling sex addicts and their partners.

Therapists Who Have Little or No Experience in Dealing with Sex Addiction

In our research with couples dealing with sexual addiction, the primary complaint was that the therapist was unfamiliar with sex addiction and that the therapist's approach prolonged the addict's denial about the extent of the problem. If you have little or no experience with sex addiction, let the couple know and be willing to address their marital problems with a therapist who is familiar with these issues. Some therapists find it useful to get peer supervision from someone familiar with sex addiction diagnosis and treatment.

High-Risk Acting Out

Sex addicts engage in a variety of behaviors that the partner may or may not view as extramarital—for example, collecting Internet pornography, telephone sex, viewing nude dancers, masturbation with another person on the computer, and sexual massage. Most sex addicts, however, do engage in behaviors that involve sexual contact with another person, often without protection from sexually transmitted diseases.

This was evident in the results of our survey, which found that of the 100 sex addict responses, 91 percent reported engaging in sexual behaviors that included another person.

Involvement with another person presents a different threat or cost to the relationship than solitary sexual activities. For one, it increases the risk that the partner will want to leave the relationship, and therefore makes it more difficult for the addict to disclose the behaviors. For another, involvement with another person risks exposure of the addict—and by extension, the partner— to sexually transmitted diseases. The risk of infection with a sexually transmitted disease, especially HIV, presents an ethical dilemma for the therapist who learns about a concealed affair. Given the ethical stipulation that therapists report to authorities when a person's life is in danger, an HIV positive addict might be asked by his or her therapist to disclose to the partner. If the addict has not yet been tested, you will want to suggest he be tested immediately.

Other Areas of Safety

In any informed consent letter or discussion, it is required by most licensure practice acts to declare to the potential client the limitations of confidentiality regarding sexual or physical abuse of a minor or others who do not have the ability to make an informed decision. The duty to report abuse and potential homicide or suicide are generally clear but can be different from state to state. Many therapists question their duty to report users of pornography. Possession of child pornography is a crime in all states but viewing is less clear. Make sure you have checked your licensure practice act and law enforcement about the requirements in your state and inform your clients prior to the first session.

If the addict or the partner fears for their physical safety, appropriate steps should be taken to get the couple to separate for a short period of time. If domestic violence has been part of the couple's history, she needs to have a back-up plan for leaving if the situation increases in volatility. Especially when it is the woman who has acted out sexually outside the marriage, the therapist needs to assess the risk of violence before recommending disclosure.

Another area of safety concerns potential victims of sexual offenders. When sexual behaviors include victimizing others, the therapist's first priority needs to be to get the client to stop the behaviors and if it involves a minor, then that offense must be reported. A significant therapist mistake is to focus on getting the addict to understand the sources of the behavior, resolve childhood trauma, etc., without directly addressing the behavior itself. When in doubt, seek consultation. If you are not skilled in this area, then referring to others who have this expertise is wise.

Another area of offending behavior that is reportable in most states is a sexual boundary violations by a licensed professional. For example, in his book *Therapists Who Have Sex with Their Patients*, Dr. Herbert Strean describes his treatment of a male therapist who over time had had sexual relations with several female clients. He relates how over a four-year period, using psychoanalytic psychotherapy, he was finally able to bring the patient to sufficient mental health that he no longer felt compelled to get his emotional needs met through sexual contact with clients. However, the issue of the trauma done to the clients and the need to immediately stop the behavior was reportedly never directly addressed, and the patient apparently continued the behavior for an extended time period while undergoing therapy. (Sexual relations with a therapy client or patient is so potentially damaging to the patient that it is prohibited by professional associations and licensing bodies throughout the United States and Canada, and is a felony in several states.)

Similarly, when a client relates to a helping professional that her partner disclosed to her some potentially victimizing sexual activities, it is a mistake to underestimate the gravity of the situation. For example, in a survey of partners of cybersex addicts, we heard from a young woman that when she was engaged to be married, her fiancé admitted he was downloading pornographic images of underage girls from the computer. She went to her minister for counseling, to discuss her options. She reported that the minister dismissed her concern, stating that her fiancé was probably "just curious," and that after they were married, his curiosity would undoubtedly be satisfied by having sex with his wife. Unfortunately, the husband's behavior continued long past the marriage, and the wife was now worried about his risk of arrest.

The bottom line is, when a client admits to behaviors that are illegal, dangerous, or involve victimizing others, therapists must make it their priority to assure the safety of the addict, spouse, and potential victims. Therapists need to be familiar with the laws of their state regarding reporting to police information the therapist received from a client regarding sexual activity involving underage children, including possession of child pornography. An excellent review was provided by Charles Samenow, in his 2012 article," Child Pornography and the Law: A Clinician's Guide." Additionally, ATSA (www.atsa.org) and SASH (www.sash.net) are two organizations that provide specialized training for the assessment and treatment of sex offenders.

Mismanaged Anger

In the past, partners were encouraged to rage through their anger, hitting mock images of the addict or perpetrator. Research has shown that this approach to helping people express their anger is usually not helpful; instead it keeps the person in a state of rage and connected to their trauma rather than released from it. It is more helpful for the partner to identify what she is angry about, note the level of anger on a scale of 0 to 10, and then make a plan for reducing her anger so that she can think clearly about any action that needs to be taken. Sometimes therapists have partners write anger letters and read them aloud, but it is important that the partner is accountable in that letter about how she contributes to the situation or makes the situation worse for herself. Finally, she should declare what would make things better for her today since nothing can be done about the past.

Premature Diagnosis

When a client presents with a sexual problem, ferreting out its cause may require some detective work. An all-too-common therapist mistake is to diagnose without obtaining an adequate sexual history of both the addict and the partner. It's all too easy to blame the partner. For example, a client who complains that her husband is not interested in sex with her may in fact have a husband who has lost interest because she has very rigid ideas about what constitutes appropriate sexual activities, and may benefit from education about common sexual practices such as oral sex or manual stimulation. Or her husband may indeed have a sexual aversion disorder or sexual dysphoric disorder (also termed sexual anorexia). However he may on the contrary be an active sex addict who is spending hours every night downloading pornography and masturbating, and that is why he is no longer interested in partner sex. If a client describes her own loss of interest in sex with her husband, she may have sexual anorexia, but alternatively she may be reacting appropriately to living with a spouse who has disclosed that he spends hours masturbating on the computer, and who, after ten years of marriage suddenly wants her to participate in unusual sexual practices with which she is uncomfortable. Take the time to ask enough questions to get a full understanding of what is happening in the relationship. When a couple has mismatched sexual interests or activities, do not hasten to diagnose the problem as an uptight, sexually uninformed, or prudish partner. Rather than instinctively blaming the wife, get a thorough history.

In other cases, the diagnosis may be correct, but the labeling may be premature. Partners are very sensitive to being labeled along with the addict. In the past we have used the term coaddict and codependent for the partner of an addict. However, through our own research and that of others and our clinical experience, such labels rarely help the partner begin to see her part in the dance. Partners report that they experience the situation as traumatic and while some of their behavior may have codependent traits, they do not find the label helpful. After the chaos begins to subside, it is easier for the partner to see that some of her behaviors have contributed to the situation with the couple. Early on, let her hear those labels at support group meetings from other partners in similar situations. Introduce the concept, if appropriate, after you (the therapist) understand the context of her situation.

Timing of Disclosure

As we have described earlier, the addict most commonly discloses initially when the partner is about to learn the truth anyway, or when the partner has already learned some incriminating information. Other addicts, however, develop so much guilt that they feel a huge buildup of pressure to unburden. At some point they may dump everything precipitously, without considering the consequences for the spouse. Although addicts often initiate therapy because their partner insists or encourages this after obtaining some information, some addicts begin therapy before their partner knows anything about their addiction. If the addict is in treatment with you, what should you do when your client wants to come clean to his unsuspecting partner, someone who has no therapist herself nor any Twelve-Step support? In our research, we heard from many partners how traumatizing it was for them to have unexpectedly been provided with painful and terrifying information when they had no support for themselves. Although we favor early disclosure for reasons we previously discussed, we recommend that you begin to plan with the addict a joint meeting with the spouse – but hold it only after she has begun to see a therapist herself. The addict can tell her that he's been working in therapy to deal with some serious problems he's had which impact the relationship, that he needs her help, that he would like her to come with him to a session with you, and that for her to have her own therapist would be a big help.

If, as is more usual, the couple comes to see you after the initial disclosure, all you can do is support and validate the partner and process the disclosure with the couple. When there is additional material to reveal, doing so in session with you is likely to be most helpful for the partner. If the addict has written a letter to the partner, process that letter in the session. Discourage the addict from disclosing or giving a letter to the partner outside the session or without you first reading it and making comments or recommendations.

Earlier in this book we discussed the adverse consequences of disclosure by an addict during treatment, at a time when the spouse has no support to deal with the effects on her of the information. If the addict is in treatment elsewhere, if the partner is not able to be with him at the center for the initial or for further divulging, arrange with the treatment center to have him reveal any further information only when she is in session with you.

Use of Outside Monitoring and Polygraph

Some therapists recommend private detectives and polygraph testing to monitor the activities of the addict. While our research has shown that partners who requested a polygraph to verify the addict's report of his or her behavior also report it as helpful to increase trust, polygraph testing needs to be used with a caution. Other than baseline verification in the truth-seeking stage early in recovery, we do not recommend this type of monitoring unless the addict agrees that it will help him remain in recovery. A couple's relationship built on this much distrust is doomed to become a reenactment of unresolved parent-child issues. At some point the partner has to be mature enough to tolerate her own discomfort of not being able to be sure of anything but herself.

Saving Face

Often the partner will declare: "If you ever do x, y, z I am leaving you." Then time goes by, the addict does well, and trust is re-established to a great degree. They recommit and everything is going well for a length of time. Then he relapses—usually not to the extent of the original acting out—but he relapses nonetheless. Now the partner is faced with her old threat. All the old memories of the original betrayal resurface as well as the pain. But now it is even harder to leave. The partner has worked hard to make changes herself and has seen changes she has liked in the addict. Now what does she do? We often invite the partner to devise some way that the addict can make restitution by taking certain actions. This may be to have HIV testing done for an extended period of time and wear a condom when they re-engage in sexual activity. Sometimes it is some gift or task he takes on.

While this may seem punitive, when the meaning of the "penance" is reframed through the partner's explanation of "this is what it takes for me to save face with myself for not leaving," the addict often views this in a different light.

Even more powerful is letting the partner discover a new perspective about the addict and herself. With this new perspective, she can change her mind.

Countertransference

Since about half of married Americans have had an affair at some point during their marriage, it is quite likely that the therapist has either had an affair or has been in a coupled relationship in which an affair happened. It is also common for therapists to have experienced an affair within their own family of origin. If you have not resolved those trust issues, then your countertransference will interfere with being objective in your approach with a couple. Seek assistance from your peer supervisor about these issues and if they persist, refer the couple to another therapist.

Personal Sharing

Although many therapists in recovery disclose some information about their history, it is not advisable to share information about your own affair or sexual acting out history with couples. This type of personal information is private and unless you and your spouse (or former spouse) have gone public with this information, you are betraying the confidentiality of your mate. It is not uncommon for clients who have a less than favorable outcome to then spread stories about you. An overly dependent client may believe that she or he is your best friend because you have shared such intimate information. It is okay to share less intimate stories that teach skills or demonstrate techniques for resolving problems, but using case examples or metaphors are more appropriate.

Don't Give Up Too Soon

It takes between two and five years for individuals to really get comfortable and do well with recovery. That may translate into many years of couple therapy as well. Couples who stop therapy in fewer than twelve sessions are more likely to separate, and the healing process is replaced with destructive interactions. Unfortunately, this leads to more stress and to increased risk of relapse for both addicted person and partner. Although most couples do not remain in weekly therapy beyond the first year or so, most who do well return to therapy from time to time for several sessions when additional difficult problems come up.

Be cautious of the couple in which the addict is quickly remorseful and attentive and the partner is swept off her feet into believing all is well. This style of interacting, common in addicted couples, is likely to lead them back to relapse when stress and anxiety return to the relationship. Gently confront the couple in which you see this wishful thinking and unrealistic "flight into health." Explain to them that the path to recovery is lengthy and at times difficult. Encourage the couple to see therapy as a long-term investment in themselves as well as their relationship.

Conclusions

Throughout this book we have emphasized our belief that disclosure is a cornerstone of healing. Most couples who have experienced disclosure agree with this statement, and recommend the process to other recovering couples. We have also pointed out the adverse consequences of revealing secrets. Clearly, there are some ways of doing this that are better than others. Therapists are in a unique position to facilitate this process for clients, to answer for them questions about the timing of disclosure, about how much to reveal, and to whom, about telling children and parents, employers, and TV talk show hosts, about situations when it might be better not to disclose, and about the difference between secrecy and privacy. But therapists need to be educated about disclosure, about its benefits and risks for couples, and about how to best facilitate. We hope this chapter has answered some of your questions about this process.

References

Samenow, Charles. Child pornography and the law: A clinician's guide. *Sexual Addiction and Compulsivity* 19:16-29, 2012.

Strean, H. *Therapists Who Have Sex With Their Patients*. New York: Brunner Mazel, 1993.

Appendix 1:

Frequently Asked Questions

Q: After three years of "sexual sobriety" from pornography, massage parlors, and prostitutes, I had a slip recently – I got on the Internet and got involved in some interactive cybersex. I told my sponsor and my Twelve-Step group, but not my wife. It took her a long time to trust me again. Should I tell her?

The short answer is yes. But more importantly, tell her what was going on for you which triggered you to want to medicate with the Internet. If it is merely that you have not yet removed the ease with which you can access this type of information on the Internet, then also tell her that you must do that.

Learning all the things that can cause you a problem takes time. Be certain that you and your mate have discussed what she wants to know and what she wants you to process with your group members, sponsor or therapist. We recommend that your partner ask to hear about if you had a bad day and what you are doing to prevent a relapse rather than wanting to know every slip you may have. If she has trouble handling your disclosure, then have a few sessions of couple therapy to determine how to manage acknowledging slips without you being punished for your honesty.

Q: After a lifetime of flirting, intrigues, and several affairs, I recently bottomed out and am beginning recovery in Sex & Love Addicts Anonymous (SLAA). I haven't said anything to my husband. I don't know if he suspects anything. He's very dependent on me, I guess very codependent, and I think he might get suicidal if I tell him the truth. What should I do?

If you feel that your mate may be suicidal, you would be wise to begin marital therapy and discuss this with your therapist in an individual session. It is very difficult to hide that you are going to meetings and working a program, so it is likely that it won't be long before he'll know something is going on. Additionally, his codependent traits needs to be addressed or the dance you both have done in the relationship is likely to return and put you at risk for relapse.

Q: My husband and I have been married 20 years. Ten years ago, when I was feeling strongly the lack of intimacy between us, I got involved in a brief affair with a coworker. After a month, I realized it wasn't the answer to my problems, and I broke it off. My husband has been recovery for a year from his sex addiction and I have been in recovery for my codependent traits. He has disclosed all of his acting-out behaviors to me. Should I tell him about this affair?

What's good for the goose is also good for the gander. If you expected him to be honest with you about his sexual acting out, then does he not also expect you to be honest about yours? If you are both in recovery, then we assume that you practice a program of rigorous honesty. Your husband might be angry and hurt when he hears about your brief affair, but the two of you will get past it. In our research, we learned that men who are themselves in recovery, especially from sex addiction, tend to be much more understanding and forgiving about a wife's affair than are other men, especially when this happened ten years ago.

Q: I saw my good buddy's wife sitting in a coffee shop with another guy. They were holding hands, and occasionally they kissed. My buddy thinks he has a great marriage. Should I tell him what I saw?

Would you want to find out from your buddy or your wife if the situation were reversed? Most people would want to hear this from their mate. Have a chat with his wife. Tell her what you saw and that you think it is her responsibility to be honest with him about the trouble in their marriage. Tell her you hope they can get help and work things out but you won't keep the secret for her. Let her know you realize that figuring out how and when to tell him isn't easy, but you will tell him in another week unless she does. Remind her that you remain a support for both of them should he or she need someone to talk to after the disclosure.

Q: My wife and I are in marriage counseling. I told my therapist about several affairs I've had over the years. I'm not involved with anyone right now. The therapist says that as long as the last affair

is over, there's no point in telling my wife, that we should focus on the present. My wife keeps blaming herself for stuff that's happened between us, which I know is at least in part because I was involved with these other women. Should I tell my wife?

We tend to agree with your therapist. Think about what kinds of things you did to create distance or give you an excuse to get out of the house. Take responsibility for your actions during the times she is blaming herself for the trouble between you. You can acknowledge what you did that contributed to the distress between you during that period, such as blaming her or criticizing her to create distance. On the other hand, if your mate has made it clear that she wants honesty between you about the past and the present, then it would be useful to tell her. Most people in marital therapy who are not dealing with addiction are encouraged to focus on the present and not hold on to old history to create chaos now.

We noticed that you haven't said you are through with affairs, just that there's no one else now. We would encourage you to look a little further with your therapist into your history of several affairs. Perhaps you are indeed dealing with an addiction, in which case you need to take additional steps for your own recovery. Those steps would include eventually sharing your past with your wife.

Q: The other day I caught my twelve-year old son looking at Internet pornography on his own computer. He doesn't know about my own problem with cybersex addiction, and I was horrified to think that he's already involved in the same behavior that almost cost me my marriage. I know that kids, especially boys, are very curious about sex, so hopefully this is just normal behavior for his age. I don't want to make a mountain out of a molehill. How do I talk to him about this without making it so forbidden that it becomes all the more attractive to him?

Think about your values. What do you want your son to know about treating women with dignity rather than making them an object? What would you say if your twelve-year-old was experimenting with alcohol? Many men in recovery speak to their adolescent sons about this issue. First they explain how people can be addicted to both drugs as well as behaviors; some then disclose their own addiction. (At some point you need to discuss your addiction because your children have your genes, thus increasing their propensity towards addiction.) Second, they acknowledge that it is normal to be curious about women's bodies and sex, but that pornography is not the best way to learn. Then they give the adolescent a few age-appropriate sexuality books or together look up more appropriate sex education sites on the computer such as those listed on www.SIECUS.org. Additionally, they remind the young man that the woman in the picture is someone's sister or daughter and ask if they would want someone looking at and having sexual thoughts or masturbating to images of his sister or daughter. This leaves the door open to further discussions of healthy masturbation, sex within a committed relationship, or any other issues that may come up.

Even if you do not disclose your addiction, it is important to tell your son that although you viewed pornography earlier in your life, you are no longer doing it because it interferes with your relationship with his mother and because it shows disrespect to women. Oh yes, be sure to tell him that you do not want him to view pornography on the computer, his cell phone or elsewhere in your home.

Q: When I was 15, I got pregnant and gave up the child for adoption. I've felt a lot of shame over the years about my early sexual behavior, and never told my husband. My daughter is now 21, and I'd very much like to try to find her. Should I tell my husband? I think my husband would forgive me for my behavior, but I also think he'd be very angry about my keeping this from him all these years. I hesitate to rock the boat when we have a very good marriage.

If you plan to try to find your daughter, most likely you will need your husband's help. If you find her and she wants to reconcile, you will undoubtedly want to share that celebration with him. You need to tell him so that he can share in your desire to find her. It sounds like you have a solid relationship. Your husband may be mad or disappointed, but if he gets to hear about your shame and fear as a teen, it seems probable that he will soon be by your side in this goal.

A friend of mine, who knew she'd been adopted at birth, began searching for her birth mother after her adoptive mother died when my friend was 40 years old. She soon found her and wrote her a letter, giving her own date of birth and hospital where she was born, but otherwise couched in sufficiently vague language that if the older woman had not told anyone, the letter wouldn't give her away. Her biological mother replied, but said she hadn't told her husband or children of her teenage pregnancy, so she hesitated to meet my friend. Shortly thereafter the woman disclosed to her husband. His reaction was to strongly encourage his wife to invite my friend to visit. As a result, my friend met her birth mother and her 4 biological sisters, whom she strongly resembles. She now has a whole new family, and her birth mother was able finally, at age 58, to let go of the shame she had felt all these years.

Q: I had treatment for cancer in my teens, and as a result I am infertile. Our daughter was conceived using sperm from another donor. Some of my family members know about this. Should we tell her that I am not her biological father? She's now 5 years old.

At some point she needs to know for medical reasons if no other. And you certainly want her to get the information from you and your wife rather than from another family member! However, at five years of age, she needs two loving parents, not information about her conception.

Q: My wife's parents don't know about my sex addiction or recovery program. As for her own recovery, she told them she been going to a "women's support group," which they think is just an opportunity for women to complain about their husbands. I'd like to be able to tell them more, but my wife is sure they'd be very judgmental and negative about me/us, and she's probably right. Should I keep them in the dark?

This is an issue that is between you and your wife. If her parents have been judgmental in the past, it may be best not to tell them. For now, this information seems to be a private matter between you and your wife. Relationships change. Overtime you both may decide you want to tell more.

Q: My husband knows about my affairs up to a year ago, when I got honest with him and started counseling. At the time he told me if I were ever unfaithful again, he'd leave me and file for custody of our two children. Since then, I've had an affair with a guy from a chat room. I'm getting help from my therapist and sponsor in SAA, but it would really hurt him and ultimately our children if I told him.

Don't you think this is what the 9th step is for – to make amends except when it would hurt others?

Men are more likely than women to leave relationships after disclosure, but in general, most partners do not leave after a relapse despite the threat to do so. It sounds like you are responding more to your shame and fear of losing him than the actual fear of hurting him and your kids – otherwise hurting them would have been a deterrent to relapse. Also, don't forget, people grow from pain and disappointment if given the opportunity. Do you want him to stay in the relationship based on misinformation, or by choice? What will be the impact if you don't tell and he finds out later? Can you remain in recovery if you do not tell him? (Clearly you were not able to remain in recovery as a result of telling and his threat!) Our experience is that you if hold onto this secret, it will fuel the rationalizations that you will later use to give yourself permission to act out. Then you are back where you started.

Q: I've been involved with prostitutes as part of my sex addiction – I just had an HIV test and it was negative. I'd rather not upset my wife unnecessarily. Should I tell her? She knows about my addiction but thinks it is pornography and go-go bars.

If you have had sex with a prostitute and then sex with your wife, then despite your negative HIV test you still may have infected her with some other type of sexually transmitted disease such as chlamydia (which often has few symptoms until it is very progressed) or Herpes. She deserves to know so that she can protect her own health. Additionally, telling one lie to cover another lie is an invitation for relapse. She will be even more upset if she finds she has a sexually transmitted disease or some other evidence that you have not been honest with her.

Q: What's the best way to tell our 15-year old daughter and 17-year old son about my sex addiction? I've been sober for three years and my wife goes to S-Anon.

Your children are old enough to know both about addiction and sexuality and are at the age in which kids are talking about both and experimenting lots. Ask them for a block of uninterrupted time for a serious talk. Both you and your wife should be present. Tell them that you want to share information that is hard for you to talk about and you realize they may not want to hear. (Most kids do not want to have this sensitive information. At the same time, they want some explanation about various things that have happened connected to your behaviors.) Because there may be a genetic link to addiction, and because most addictive behavior begins in adolescence, they need to know so that they can be aware of the warning signs of any addiction. Remind them that people can become addicted to behaviors as well as substances. Disclose that you are a recovering addict and that your drug of choice has been sex. Tell them that you've been honest with their Mom about what you have done in your sex addiction. Often in first conversations, specific information is omitted, especially with younger children. However, if you and your wife agree on the content, you may give teenagers more information, leaving out specific details. For example,

"I got involved with viewing pornography and compulsive mastur-bation. While masturbation is healthy for some people, for me it was a way I used to escape and to avoid feeling anything."

Here is a chance for you to talk about the values that guide your recovery. "I also want to say that I now feel strongly that most of the time pornography objectifies women and does not provide any real opportunity for learning how to be with other people, much less solve problems. I feel bad about how I used it. It took me away from Mom and caused problems in our relationship."

Mom might chime in here about her codependent traits if she has them. It may be useful to say that experimental use of certain 'adult' behaviors or drugs to alter your mood is common among young peo-ple, but kids who have addiction in their background need to be careful not to fall into the trap of believing this is a solution to their problems.

Now ask if they have any questions or want to say anything. Be quiet and give them a chance to get beyond the discomfort of speaking about this. To end, tell them if they ever have any questions to let you or their Mom know. Tell them that you love them. Do take opportunities to bring this up again so it becomes easier for everyone to talk about.

Q: I've been sober from my bottom-line of cybersex for six months, but I haven't been able to stop the masturbation yet. Do I need to tell my wife every time I masturbate? (See section on healthy masturbation.)

After your initial disclosure, it is important for couples to decide what to share. Early on, partners usually do want to know when someone has had a slip and what the addict is trying to do to stay in recovery. It is important that she not measure her self-worth by your ability to remain sober. (A period of abstinence from masturbation is useful and important for you as an addict. Some addicts are able to return to a healthy form of masturbation at a later date, but not all.) You must also discuss how you can be honest and not get punished for your honesty. Everyone must learn to deal with their own anxiety in the early stages of recovery from addiction, the trauma of betrayal, and codependent traits..

Q: My boss is beginning to give me heat because I leave so often to go to counseling and psychotherapy appointments. How much should I tell him about my sex addiction?

Unless you have a close working relationship with your boss, telling is risky. Telling anyone at work has to be weighed against the odds that the information will be misused or that you may get fired. If you feel your job would be in jeopardy, you may have to adjust your therapy schedule or arrange to work extra hours before or after work. If you are a valued employee and you feel you have a good working relationship with your boss, then disclose only general information and the need to continue in therapy. If you can be specific about how much time you will need off, that is usually helpful to your boss.

Q: I'm caught between wanting and not wanting to tell my minister about my sex addiction. He keeps requesting that I volunteer for Youth Group work. I have an attraction to teen-age girls but haven't acted on any of those fantasies. What would be the best way to handle this?

If you have been part of the congregation for some time and feel that you have a good relationship with the minister, then disclosure will help you be firm in your boundaries and may help educate the minister who is in position to help others. On the other hand, if few people know you and this is your first community service, request some other type of volunteer position until you are better known and you get to know the minister better. He should be bound to confidentiality, but in the event any teen made a complaint, you will probably be the first to be blamed.

Q: I am gay and my sponsor says the only sobriety is to be abstinent. I am not okay with this. Should I change sponsors or is he right? My Twelve-Step group agrees with this.

There are several different Twelve-Step programs for sex addiction; some are a better fit for gays and lesbians. Some Twelve-Step groups do believe that if you are not in a legal marriage, abstinence is the only way to recovery. As same-sex marriages is still illegal in most states, marriage cannot determine sobriety for gay and lesbian couples any more than it can for straight couples. However, some period of abstinence is important for all recovering addicts. Most gay men determine that after a period of recovery, they want to develop a set of guidelines for healthy sexual experimentation and expression. This might include something like sex only in a committed relationship, or no sex with strangers and no use of any type of mood-altering drug or alcohol during sex. You must decide for yourself what is healthy gay behavior, but that is very hard to do without input from others early in recovery. Get some advice from other gay men with some lengthy and good recovery about how they have dealt with this. You may want to find a gay sponsor if possible. You might also want to find a different Twelve-Step program.

Q: I just got married. My wife knows about my sex addiction and is very supportive of my recovery. She does not know my whole past history especially the cyber-relationship I had with another woman when I was married before. How much does she need to know now?

Unless you agreed to tell her all about your past, or unless you have already relapsed or slipped or are fearful for your recovery by keeping this from her, what is in the past is not as important as what you share now.

Appendix 2:

Recovery Resources

I. Twelve-Step Resources

These mutual-help programs have meetings in many locations throughout the U.S. and some other countries. They also have online reading material, information about location of meetings, and some have online meetings.

12-step programs for Sex Addicts
Sexaholics Anonymous
e-mail: saico@sa.org
www.sa.org
Tel: (615) 370-6062

Sex & Love Addicts Anonymous
www.slaafws.org
(210) 828-7900

Sex Addicts Anonymous
e-mail: info@saa-recovery.org
web: www.sexaa.org/
(800) 477-8191
(713) 869-4902

Sexual Compulsives Anonymous (SCA)
web: www.sca-recovery.org
Tel: (800) 977-HEAL

Sexual Recovery Anonymous (SRA)
email: info@sexualrecovery.org
www.sexualrecovery.org

For the Partner or Family Member:
Codependents of Sex Addicts (COSA)
email: info@cosa-recovery.org
www.cosa-recovery.org
866) 899-COSA (2672)

S-Anon International Family Groups
email: sanon@sanon.org
www.sanon.org
(615)833-3152
800) 210-8141

For teenage family members of sexual addicts:
S-Ateen
Contact: S-Anon International Family Groups

For Couples
Recovering Couples Anonymous (RCA)
email: wso-rca@recovering-couples.org
website: www.recovering-couples.org
877-663-2317
(781) 794-1456

For Sexual Trauma Survivors:
Survivors of Incest Anonymous (SIA)
website: siawso.org
(410) 893-3322

Incest Survivors Anonymous (ISA)
website: lafn.org
Tel: (562) 428-5599

For Sex Workers:
Sex Workers Anonymous
(702) 612-1253

II.Other Resources

Society for the Advancement of Sexual Health (SASH)
email: SASH@SASH.net
website: www.sash.net
(770) 541-9912

The Society for the Advancement of Sexual Health (SASH) is a non-profit multidisciplinary organization dedicated to scholarship, training, and resources for promoting sexual health and overcoming problematic sexual behaviors (sex addiction, hypersexual disorder, out of control sexual behavior, sexual impulsivity, sexual abuse.) The website contains educational material including position papers, contact information for Twelve-Step programs, and a list of relevant books, as well as contact information for knowledgeable sex addiction therapists all over the U.S and internationally. SASH sponsors an academic journal, *Sexual Addiction and Compulsivity: The Journal of Treatment and Prevention,* and also an annual conference.

Straight Spouse Network
www.ssnetwk.org

Index

Made in the USA
San Bernardino, CA
09 June 2014